In Pursuit of Freedom and Justice

In Pursuit of Freedom and Justice

A Memoir

Cephas G. Msipa

Published by
Weaver Press, Box A1922, Avondale, Harare. 2015
<www.weaverpresszimbabwe.com>

© Cephas George Msipa

Typeset by Weaver Press
Cover photograph: Wide Angle
Cover Design: Danes Design, Harare
Map: Street Savvy
Printed by: Directory Publishers, Bulawayo

Photograph on pp. 28, 67, 96 courtesy of the National Ar-
chives and the Ministry of Information in Zimbabwe.
All other photographs from the author's private collection.

ISBN: 978-1-77922-282-4

Acknowledgements

I am deeply appreciative of my family and friends for their help, time, advice, support and encouragement as I worked on this memoir. My sons worked long and arduously on my story to ensure that the details were as correct as we could make them and that the text had a sequential flow.

My heartfelt gratitude to Primrose Faku and Tsitsi Muchohonyi my administrative assistants, who worked for many hours to research some of the material and to do the original typing of the manuscript from my dictation.

My good friends Professor Ngwabi Bhebhe, Professor Rungano Jonas Zvobgo and Dr Hazel Ngoshi have been very generous with their time in reading and commenting on earlier drafts of the book.

Many other people have rendered invaluable assistance to me in compiling these reminiscences and reflections. To them all I express my sincere appreciation.

I dedicate this book to my parents, Elijah and Anne Msipa,
for nurturing and believing in me and for their support, guidance
and love for me and for my brothers and sisters.
I can never repay the debt of gratitude I owe to
my wife, Charlotte Sithabile Msipa, who stood by me through
thick and thin and with whom I shared my life and adventures for
over 55 years until her death in April 2013.

FOREWORD

It was in Gweru, in mid-2008, that I first had a personal encounter with Cephas Msipa. Prior to that, he had been a political figure I saw on television, read about in the newspapers or met in banking halls where he would humbly join the queues like everybody else. I had always admired the gentility and sobriety of character. The circumstances of my meeting him were purely academic. I was young and my academic career was in its infancy. When a faculty meeting at the local university proposed that we confer an honorary doctorate on a distinguished individual, Cephas Msipa's name was the first one suggested. In my youthful excitement, I volunteered to write the proposal for the citation since I had access to some historical material a colleague was working on. Through one of his aides, Msipa came to know about me and we were introduced to each other. Even though the honorary doctorate was later conferred by the Faculty of Commerce, my contact with him had been established. He struck me as a fatherly figure. I did not attend the graduation ceremony where the doctorate was conferred, but a colleague told me of how he had looked for me everywhere – to be with him and President Mugabe for a photo session.

This relationship and the fact that I had told Dr Msipa of my intention to undertake doctoral studies with a focus on autobiography partly provided the impetus for this his autobiography. I say partly because he has always been clear about his motivations for writing a memoir:

> I want to leave a record hoping those coming after me
> may benefit from my experiences in detention, the lib-

> *eration struggle and what we went through, lest peo-*
> *ple may forget. I want to continue to talk to people*
> *even after I am dead. I am putting myself on the line to*
> *say here: 'I am, this is what I have said and hear what*
> *people will say'.*

He has often added, "I know Robert more intimately than most
people do." Those who respect his political culture have also been
nagging him for his story:

> *What motivated me most was that people I spoke to,*
> *both black and white, urged me to write about my long*
> *journey from Rhodesia to Zimbabwe. The period be-*
> *tween 1957 and 1980 was of great political signifi-*
> *cance as it brought an end to colonialism.*

The result is a story of personal contribution to the liberation of
Zimbabwe, and the public and private sectors of this country. It is
a story about his family and childhood, which shaped his dreams,
and the colonial experiences including detention that sharpened
those dreams and the struggle to fulfil them. It is the story of an
honest man.

Cephas Msipa's character is unassuming, but his life has been
extraordinary in many regards, mainly because of a professional
and political career that spans close to six decades. He belongs to
the generation of illustrious Zimbabweans who fought for our independence and went on to contribute to the nation-building process. What separates him from his peers is the level-headedness
and sincerity of his political praxis. As a politician, he has always
acted above the fray and his contributions have always been carefully considered. If there is ethics in politics, he is best qualified to
personify ethical politics.

This book is the story of multi-layered narratives of life lived
as a young man struggling to earn an education; it recounts the
growth in political consciousness of a young and dedicated educa-

tionist who becomes increasingly politically aware due to the ways in which the Rhodesian state oppressed black people. He claims in the narrative that he was "a teacher by profession and politician by circumstance". The book also contains an alternative narrative of post-independent Zimbabwe in which he articulates a version of political developments in the early days of our nation – initially from a ZAPU perspective and later from a ZANU-PF insider's perspective. Msipa articulates the intrigues of the early days of Zimbabwe – the conflicting agendas for the new nation, the dark episode of Gukurahundi and the ensuing political compromises that had to be made – with a candour that belies his diplomatic personality. Perhaps, again, Msipa is one politician to talk about Zimbabwean politics and he does so without rancour. Written in simple, accessible language, the narrative addresses in some detail, the most important milestones in the political history of this country.

Msipa also takes us through the rich tapestry of his personal life as it interweaves with the nation's history. There is no artificiality or affectation as he chronicles his political culture and his idea of service within both the public and private sectors of Zimbabwe. His political culture is distinct from that of some of his colleagues. He writes that he "vowed never to use violence as a political tool" after observing the culture of fear among our people. The narrative is equally introspective as he revisits his role in nation-building. The question that haunted him while in the public sector, and still does, is, "Why are we so poor?" This is in view of the fact that Zimbabwe remains poor despite being richly endowed with abundant resources that could benefit its people.

To put it mildly, the general feeling today is that we are fast approaching the end of an era (the era of old nationalist politicians). Msipa has repeatedly told me: "You see, I am old now, my days are numbered, I need to finish this book. If I die now, some things will be left untold." If this is true, then there is urgent need, today, for documenting Zimbabwe's past in autobiography. There is therefore real virtue in Msipa's book, especially for historians and theorists of autobiography.

For readers who crave for multiple stories of our nation, for backgrounds against which the question of the trajectories followed, Msipa's life is a near-unique case. The book not only informs, but educates, and will no doubt stir debate.

Msipa's narrative has taught me a great deal and I have no hesitation in recommending it. My regrets at not having known him longer are mitigated in this book and the reasons for his being awarded the honorary Doctor of Commerce by the Midlands State University have been illuminated.

Hazel Tafadzwa Ngoshi, Ph.D.
Chairperson, Dept. of Literature,
Midlands State University.

October, 2015.

Preface

This is a book by one who has walked through the armed struggle, experienced the brutality of the colonial system at first hand. One who witnessed families being separated by the colonial system. It is a lucid exploration of the journey of an African freedom fighter, Cde Cephas Msipa.

This book falls within specific periods; the first stage is Cde Msipa's early years as a teacher, a member of the African Teachers Association and the early years of the formation of his political vision. The second stage chronicles his years in Kwekwe and Highfields where he was already playing a prominent role in politics. He remained the bridge between ZAPU leaders out of the country and supporters in the country. The final stage is the post cease fire period, years as minister in government and the various roles he played in government.

Through this journey Cde Msipa highlights his arrests, the detention of African leaders and what they were struggling for. He was a ZAPU and ZANU mediator who brought the two parties together. The unity that ensued was a result of his actions as he persuaded Cde Joshua Mqabuko Nyongolo Nkomo to be in line with the President, Cde Robert Gabriel Mugabe.

This book is a milestone contribution to the knowledge body of Zimbabwe's history and heritage. A must read for everyone and anyone for whom history is an essential process that should be analysed and understood in order to make sense of the present and the future.

Rungano Jonas Zvobgo
Vice-Chancellor
University of Great Zimbabwe
October, 2015.

Map of Zimbabwe

1

My Early Years

I was born on 7 July, 1931, the first born in a family of ten children, in Shabani district in the Midlands Province under Chief Masunda. Of the ten, seven were boys and three girls. At the time of writing, four boys and one girl have left us. Those remaining are very close and we meet as family members from time to time. Our own children have maintained that relationship as well. All in all, I have eight children, thirty-one grandchildren and seven great-grandchildren.

As I look back, I am happy that I have lived for so long. Many of my friends including those I was incarcerated with in detention camps and prisons are gone. May their souls rest in peace. I suffered with them, but we also had moments of joy as we celebrated our freedom and independence on 18 April, 1980. It is a pity they missed one big celebration, that was on 3 December, 2009 when Midlands State University honoured me. It is a day I shall never forget. It was a most humbling experience, a great honour indeed. The citation read, "Doctor of Commerce in Strategic Management and Corporate Governance *Honoris Causa*" and the President of Zimbabwe and Chancellor of the Midlands State

University, capped me.

I said to myself then, what a pity some of my closest friends had been taken away from this world, including my parents who had worked so hard to have me educated when they themselves were not. Among these friends were Ariston Chambati, formerly Zimbabwe's ambassador to Germany and research officer in the International Affairs Division of the Commonwealth Secretariat, and Willie Musarurwa, the first African editor of *The Sunday Mail* and former Secretary for Publicity for PF ZAPU. These two and I, together with George Kahari, formerly a headmaster, now Professor of African Languages and Literature at the University of Zimbabwe, used to be called "the Big Four" in PF ZAPU, the party we belonged to. Death has separated me and George from Ariston and Willie, and that is the law of nature. We don't choose when to go. The Almighty keeps that power for Himself.

My parents were poor peasants, but hardworking and diligent. My father, Elijah, was born in Belingwe district in 1909 and died in early 1972. When he was only three years old, his mother died, leaving him and his young brother, Jeremiah, who was two months old. My grandfather had several wives and my grandmother was the youngest. She was born and bred in Insiza District, Matabeleland South. In accordance with our culture, after her death my maternal grandparents were invited to take their daughter's two sons and look after them. My father and his brother were looked after by their aunt as orphans in Insiza. At this tender age, they were cut off from their blood relatives in Belingwe and went to live in a new environment. Their aunt was a teenager, and how she nurtured them, particularly Jeremiah, was a wonder. A crisis arose when their aunt decided to get married. She said there was no way she could take the two kids to her new husband. No one can explain to me why my father and brother could not go back to Belingwe. Instead they were handed over to their uncle, their mother's brother-in-law, in Shabani. Life was a serious struggle for the two orphans. When I was born, there were four of us, my father and his brother, and my mother, Anne, and me. From time to time my father and his brother used to go to Mahlebadza in Belingwe and a number of our relatives there used to visit us. Even now, they call on us and regard me as one of them. In Belingwe, most of our relatives, including my Gumbo brothers, Joram and Rugare, use the Shona surname, Gumbo (leg), which is Msipa (muscle/ligament) in Ndebele. As a matter of fact, Mnene Hospital in the district was named after my great-grandfather who welcomed the Lutheran church and allowed them to establish a mission in Belingwe in 1908. His name was Mnenegwa Gumbo but the missionaries shortened it to Mnene in appreciation of his granting them permission to establish a church, school and hospital. My mother grew up in Chibi in Victoria Province. We did not have much contact with her side of the family. However, she used to go with me to Insiza nearly every year to visit my grandmother whom she regarded as her mother-in-law. The relationship was very warm and strong. My father and his brother were orphans in the true sense. From early ages they learned what it was to have no permanent home. The experience taught them to be resilient and to get along in this world.

Although my parents were very poor, having come from humble beginnings, they had a clear vision for their children. I will always remember and admire them for that. Both of them were hardworking and as a result we never went hungry. They had many friends. You could not tell that my father grew up in Matabeleland South and my mother in Chibi in Masvingo Province, as usually people who come from other districts are considered foreigners and are not easily adopted into local society. What I learnt from my parents is humility and generosity and, above all, respect for others, especially those who were older than they were.

We were inundated with visitors, mostly from Belingwe. My father, a popular figure and influential farmer in the area, had many friends, including Chief Masunda and the well-known political figure, Benjamin Burombo, from Bulawayo. Each time he was in Shabani, he would spend two or three days at our home.

Burombo's mission was very clear; he was vehemently opposed to the forced removal of Africans from their homes. He formed an organisation called the British African National Voice Association. He addressed meetings throughout the country. He appealed to the British to stop the white Rhodesian government from taking from the black people their God-given right to land, but to no avail.

When Burombo was in Shabani, my father used to accompany him to these meetings and at night they would review their successes and failures. Here was a nationally important man, sleeping on the hard floor in the same hut with my father and being satisfied with whatever my mother cooked. I was young then, but I heard Burombo and my father talk with emotion and anger. Burombo was a man of the people, and a true nationalist. I hope that some day his role is recognised and that he be re-buried at Heroes Acre, the shrine in Harare for those declared heroes of the liberation struggle. I learnt a lot from him and he was my political mentor. He had little education but his passion for downtrodden people endeared him to thousands of black people. Had the white minority Rhodesian government listened to Benjamin Burombo, we would not have experienced the years of war and struggle, on both sides, that came as a consequence of blacks being denied their rights. In many ways, what white commercial farmers have been experiencing since 2000 under President Mugabe's seizures of white-owned land, is what blacks experienced in the late 1940s under the Land Apportionment Act.[1] I am glad I got involved in

---

1   Effectively two Acts, the first passed in 1930 and the second in 1941 which strengthened the provisions of the first. It divided the country into

the resettlement programme after 2000. When I was governor in the Midlands, I supported the aspirations of the indigenous people of Zimbabwe without violence, and those like Benjamin Burombo must be smiling in their graves.

My father took up farming very seriously and was one of the first in Shabani to be awarded a Master Farmer's certificate in recognition of his knowledge and practice of modern farming methods. To get the certificate, he went through a rigorous test, which included proving that he followed crop rotation, constructed contour ridges, made use of fertilizers and planted his crops on time. In addition to farming, he was buying and selling chickens to butcheries in Shabani town. This earned him the nickname, Madendere, "the carrier of chicken nests" in Shona. He was also a small-scale businessman in his own right. From what he told me and what I saw, life for him and his young brother Jeremiah was a real struggle, a struggle for shelter, food and life itself. He inherited nothing because he was an orphan. He managed to succeed through hard work.

My father was an extremely kind man; it was no wonder he had so many friends. He beat me only once in his life. I think he had no choice. I once pretended I was going to school, but I just went halfway and waited for others to come back after school and joined them. One day my father followed me and found me asleep. It was around 10 a.m. I had never known my father to be so angry. I hated going to school, particularly during the first two years, but I changed my attitude towards schooling after that. For my earliest education, I had enrolled at Siboza Primary School, a satellite school established by Dadaya Mission, and then completed primary education at Dadaya Mission itself, which was under the New Zealand Churches of Christ. I did my primary, secondary and teacher training at Dadaya. Siboza was a day school but man-

---

"Native reserves" and "European Areas" and racially segregated urban areas. Many thousands of blacks were evicted from their homes to make way for white farmers.

aged to be very famous for its quality of education. Some students came from as far as Mhondoro in Mashonaland West to attend, and my parents looked after them. The headmaster, Wenning Moraka, was my father's friend and he managed to persuade my parents to give board and lodging to the boys to whom he had offered places. The headmaster ended up in one of the few seats reserved for blacks in the Southern Rhodesian parliament. He was clever and influential and mentored me in the early years of my teaching career.

I took a break from Dadaya in 1950 when I was forced to do temporary teaching to raise school fees for my sister Hlale, who was doing Standard 6 there. A year later she was employed as an untrained temporary teacher and made a contribution towards my school fees before she also went back to school to become a qualified teacher.

Dadaya was about 12 miles from my home but on the other side of Dadaya Mountain. We walked to the Mission carrying our luggage – including a trunk, bedding and mats – on our heads, because there was no transport. It catered mostly for children from poor families. Sir Garfield Todd and his wife, Lady Grace, started the school on their ranch, Hokonui, in Shabani in 1934.

Looking back, I can't help being mindful of the fact that I became what I am because of Dadaya Mission under the Todds. The school moved with the times. I came across missionaries from New Zealand and Australia who, in addition to general teaching, emphasised the importance of moral values. I learnt to live happily with students from all over Zimbabwe. This called for understanding, tolerance and respect of other people. The influence of the Todds has continued throughout my life. Sir Garfield was knighted by the Queen of England in recognition of his services to Africa and New Zealand. The Todds ran the school on their own for many years before other missionaries joined them. Lady Grace was an educationist whose influence was felt throughout the country because of her "Dadaya Schemes", which laid out in detail the work to be covered day by day and week by week throughout the school year.

Sir Garfield rose from the position of school principal to become prime minister of Southern Rhodesia during the days of the Federation of Rhodesia and Nyasaland. As head of the school during the Second World War, he used to tell us in school assembly why the rest of the world was fighting Adolf Hitler, and that racism was evil. He updated us on the progress of the forces fighting against the Nazis. In the process we learnt to appreciate democratic values. Sir Garfield was far ahead of most other whites, politically and socially, and in turn they considered him a threat to their lifestyles. Before long, his Cabinet and white voters accused him of advancing black people "too quickly". His Cabinet revolted against him and the white electorate voted him out in 1958. In Shabani, Africans mourned and prayed on hearing of his ouster. They loved him dearly and considered him their man as he lived with them, even assisting mothers to deliver their babies.

He identified completely with blacks and was a friend and advisor to nationalists, including Joshua Nkomo. Smith's Rhodesian Front party treated him brutally, in the same way they treated African nationalists. He underwent detention without trial and was treated as a traitor. But he joined us at the Lancaster House Conference and after independence in 1980 was appointed a senator in Zimbabwe's first black majority parliament.

In January 1972, Sir Garfield was detained in Gatooma Prison for five weeks and was subsequently restricted to his farm. His daughter, Judy, spent a similar period of imprisonment in Marandallas, also followed by house arrest; she left the country in July, but was still regarded as a detainee, and only returned in February 1980, when all detention orders were revoked by Lord Soames, the last British governor.

I think he deserved more from us, considering the suffering he underwent. Had PF ZAPU, Joshua Nkomo's party to which I belonged, won the 1980 elections, we would have appointed him a minister, I believe. At his funeral at Dadaya, I described his contribution to the country as "immeasurable". He was a man of great vision.

I am very proud of having been educated at Dadaya. It has produced many outstanding leaders and administrators, including Ndabaningi Sithole, the first leader of ZANU, Misheck Sibanda, the permanent secretary in the President's office, Simbarashe Mumbengegwi, the long-serving minister of foreign affairs, and Charles Hungwe, a judge in the High Court. I have been chairman of the Dadaya school board of governors for 24 years and only recently stepped down. The school's motto is "Education for Life", a message we have tried to instill in all those who pass through our hands. We attend to their spiritual, physical, and intellectual needs – the soul, the spirit, the body and the mind are all taken care of. This is what Sir Garfield wanted.

The school curriculum includes not only academic subjects but also practical subjects, like building and carpentry for boys and sewing and cooking for girls.

The land on which the school is built was donated by the Todds. In appreciation of the contribution these two people made to the development of Dadaya Mission in particular, and to African education generally, we built and named the administration block the "Todd Building".

As Sir Garfield grew into old age, he approached me as chairman and asked to be allowed to dig two graves, one for his wife and the other one for himself. I put it to the Board amd we agreed. Sir Garfield and Lady Grace are buried in the Dadadaya Mission cemetery. They worked at the school they loved for many years. We shall always remember them.

***

My first teaching post was in 1953 at Msipani primary school in Shabani which was under the supervision of Dadaya, and where I raised the number of classes to Standard 4. The following year I was returned to Siboza School of my childhood so I could teach closer to home before moving to urban schools. Teaching in the rural areas was a real challenge, but was also most rewarding. School children walked long distances and were poorly clothed. There were no textbooks. Classrooms were built by parents, but were of poor quality. The children were hungry but eager to learn. Accommodation for teachers consisted of thatched mud huts which leaked during the rainy season. Despite the poor environment, many students made it in life and ended up as nurses and teachers. While teaching at Msipani, I did my Senior Certificate, which was equivalent to A-level, by correspondence. I was literally studying by candlelight. Each time I visit these two schools now, I feel nostalgia when I see some of the classrooms in whose construction I participated. They are still in use. But to my very serious regret, the streams that used to flow throughout the year, which were our source of water for gardening, are dry, and so are the springs. Teachers can no longer teach gardening like we used to. Soil erosion has taken its toll.

While still at Dadaya, I was among a group of students who were given an extraordinary opportunity. In 1946, Sir Garfield and Lady Grace gave those of us who had passed Standard 4 with distinctions the chance to write Standard 5 examinations immediately afterwards, instead of at the end of the year. When we turned up for Standard 6 the next year, we were told that we were going to Form 1 – we skipped two years, and were surprised and excited by the big leap from Standard 4 to Form 1. The teachers, on the other hand, were sceptical. The Ministry of African Education tried to resist our rapid promotion, but the Todds went ahead. This was their way of advancing young Africans.

That year, in 1947, we found ourselves sitting for two examinations, Standard 6 as required by the Ministry and Form 1. It was a disaster for the majority of us but I and a few others passed both examinations. I saved my parents the problem of paying fees for Standards 5 and 6 but I don't think that they understood how well I had done. If they did, they showed no reaction or excitement – indeed, no appreciation at all. However, I was not discouraged because I knew they did not understand what my promotion meant. For me, it was a great relief, considering that during the school holidays I used to work at Sir Garfield's farm for my school fees.

***

In 2004, as my mother was growing very old, and a few months before she passed on, I asked how far she had gone with her schooling, and why she was so determined to make sure that we were all educated. She said, "I don't know for how long I was in school, perhaps a year or two.

"But as to your second question, your father and I watched how your uncle Joram, who was a building instructor at Dadaya, lived, and we agreed that the best thing we could do for our children was to have them educated." He had been educated and as a result was better-off in later life. I thanked her most sincerely. My parents had worked hard and made sacrifices to put all ten of us through school, to the point where others laughed at them for depriving themselves of so many things. But as a family, we led the way in education. My parents were torch-bearers and all my brothers and sisters will always remember them for this great heritage.

My mother was full of compassion and she showed love for all her children, and for her grandchildren as well. Alhough she spent her last days in bed, she followed what was happening, particularly with the HIV/AIDS pandemic and the unprecedented drought of 1990/91. She did not hesitate to warn me of the dangers of AIDS, as it affected elderly people in the rural areas because they had to take charge of whole families whose parents had died. Two of her children died of AIDS.

Although I was PF ZAPU, I discovered in 1987 that my mother was a ZANU(PF) supporter. From 1980 to 1987, she had insisted every month that I give her money for church offering and "the party subscription". I did not ask her which party she was supporting, assuming that it was my party. I asked her why she did not tell me that the subscriptions were going to ZANU(PF). Her reply was simple and straightforward: "I did not want to disappoint you, and I feared you would not give me the money." I laughed and said, "If you were not my mother, I would punish you for lying to me." She explained why she supported Mugabe and his party, ZANU(PF), and not Nkomo and PF ZAPU. She spoke freely and truthfully, and we laughed. I blamed politics for instilling fear in our people, including our parents. I vowed never to use fear as a political tool, and I have kept that vow.

I believe firmly that I am what I am, firstly, because of the teachings of my parents, and secondly, the influences of other forces, such as the school I attended and the people I met in my long journey. At Dadaya Mission, the school regulations forced us to communicate in English from 6 a.m. on Monday to 1 p.m. on Saturday. It was a punishable offence to speak in a vernacular language. No wonder I am not very proficient in Shona or Ndebele.

2

Urban Life and Political Activism

Two years after I had completed my teacher training course in 1952, I asked Peter Nathan, the school superintendent of the Church of Christ in Shabani, when I was going to be promoted to the position of headmaster, as I had higher qualifications than most of my peers. He said I needed to gain some experience, but how long it would take, he did not say. I told him I could not wait indefinitely and bade him goodbye. In those days teachers with my qualifications were scarce and we were much sought after.

I contacted my uncle and school classmate, Pierce Mpofu, who was teaching at Mambo Government School in Gwelo, and he advised me to come there immediately. At the Gwelo education ministry offices I was told to go to Que Que, where the government was opening a primary school in a new township, Amaveni. That marked my movement from rural schools and rural life to an urban existence. Our headmaster, a Mr Greenfield, was an Englishman. I started complaining about his behaviour as our relationship was like that of master and servant. Little did I know that some of my fellow black teachers – my "black brothers" – would report to him what I had been saying about him. I should have expected this, because this kind of behaviour was common in those days. Greenfield lacked the courage to confront me personally, and instead called a staff meeting in which he accused me of causing disharmony in the school. He likened the situation to a football team with the captain instructing the players to kick the ball up front, and another telling them to kick to the rear. Most of the teachers were puzzled, because they did not know what his outburst was about. After the meeting I asked for an audience, which he readily gave. I asked why he did not speak to me personally instead of doing it indirectly at a staff meeting. He said, "What makes you think I was talking about you?" I replied, "That's what I have been saying to some of the teachers and they agree with me." He went red and was angry. "You want to be headmaster of this school?" I said, "If I am appointed, why not?" He told me I was asking for trouble, and I said that it was my concern, and it was for the Ministry to decide what to do. He ordered me out of his office and for three weeks we did not talk to each other.

Then one day he called me to his office and handed me a letter. It was from the head office of the Ministry of Education. It was brief and it advised both of us to work together in the interest of the school. I assured him I was prepared to do that as long as he treated me and the other teachers as colleagues. We worked together like this for four years and when in 1958 the Ministry wrote to tell me that I had been transferred to Shingirayi School in Salisbury he protested and said he did not want me to leave. I was excited to move to Salisbury, as it was much bigger than Que Que. But it really touched me that we were able to part as friends.

Moving from a rural area to an urban setting was quite an unsettling experience. I knew no one outside the school. Cooking was a problem, and so was accommodation. I was only 24 years old when I arrived in Que Que, very single and very green and unprepared for life in town.

Amongst the teachers there were two pretty young ladies who had completed their teachers' training at Tegwani Methodist School in Matabeleland South. Que Que had no Church of Christ, which was my church at the time. One of the girls went to the Anglican Church while the other went to the Methodist Church. Each of them was keen for me to join her at her church and this presented a problem. People were watching to see which I would attend, as it would indicate which girl I fancied. I ended up not going to church at all.

However, before long I settled on one of the girls, Charlotte Sithabile Matabela. I later married her in 1960. She was everything that I desired in a woman. Her parents treated me like their son and I felt that I could never have better in-laws than these. They were God-fearing, welcoming, humble and respectful. Their behaviour was reflected in all their children. Before I came to live in town, my impression of people living there was that they could not be trusted and that most of them were decadent. I was proved wrong and soon I realised that the good and bad are in town and in rural areas alike. What an eye-opener.

It did not take me long to get to know Que Que. At Amaveni School, book salesmen came to us, offering us their ranges of textbooks. One of these was a big, charismatic and self-confident young man named Joshua Nkomo, who was selling the Encyclopaedia Britannica. I bought a set of ten. He impressed me with his size and jovial personality. He was travelling with his friend, Scotting Chingatie, who was of Malawian origin. Little did I know that three years later, Nkomo would be back with a new role and clear mission – as a politician and president of the Southern Rhodesia African National Congress. He had become serious as he tried to win people's hearts. I quickly established myself as the spokesman of the African people of Que Que, as I had been elected as a member and then chairman of the town's African Advisory Board. I had been elected because of my open criticism of the lack of amenities and facilities in the town – despite having gold mines dotted everywhere. The town councillors did not care to know how their workers lived as long as they came to work. The white councillors' qualifications were the colour of their skins and their promise to safeguard white interests.

It was there that I established myself as a fighter against oppression and a believer in African emancipation. My doctor in the town, Dr Isaac Hirsch, was a member of the federal parliament, and he said to me once, in 1958, "I have mixed feelings about your Joshua Nkomo but I admire him – he has made the African realise in a short space of time that he is a full human, like people of other races, and must therefore enjoy full human rights." He went on to explain how the Jews suffered at the hands of Hitler and likened the situation to that of Africans in Rhodesia where they were subjected to discrimination everywhere simply because they were black.

As a teacher, I lived in an area called Kuma Four-Four, meaning a house shared by four people with a communal toilet and showers. Between 1955 and 1958 I was in everything and everywhere. I was founder of a football team which we named "Springbok" and which produced national players such as Richard Chimenya and administrators like Nelson Chirwa. I was also on the board of the Southern Rhodesia Football Association, representing Midlands Province. I became a part-time reporter for the *Daily News* with Nathan Shamuyarira as editor-in-chief. As a reporter I rubbed shoulders with a wide cross-section of people. I recall that Regis Makaya, a candidate for Federation Prime Minister Roy Welensky's party, blamed his loss in parliamentary elections on a report I wrote which portrayed him as "a white man's stooge". He drove all the way from Salisbury and threatened to beat me up.

The majority of the people liked me for writing of the happenings in Que Que, particularly soccer, boxing and beauty contests. The advisory board managed to get the town council to establish a new township, Mbizo, in spite of stiff resistance from whites who objected to having Africans living nearby, on the eastern side of their residential areas. They only agreed after I threatened to organise a strike action. They knew we could do it because we had popular support behind us, and the support of Aaron Ndabambi Dlomo, who was President of the Railway Workers' Union, another Amaveni resident.

When it was time to leave Que Que in 1958, I was sad to go. It was now my second home, and the town which I had helped to put on the map. It is the town that inspired me, and particularly put me on track with politicians, trade unionists and, more importantly, the ordinary man, the silent majority. Two years later, I was to come back to marry Charlotte Matabela, who was later described by my dear friend, the late Willie Musarurwa, as "somebody given to you by Jesus Christ". This did not go down well with Willie's wife who asked him, "Who gave me to you?" Willie replied, "I don't know, but what I know is that it was not Jesus Christ."

Deep in my heart I knew Charlotte was special in every respect and I shall always remember the vows we made at St Martin's Church in Amaveni on 27 April, 1960, our beautiful wedding reception in Amaveni beer hall, and a second one at the Msipa family homestead in Siboza. I pray that God be with her until we meet again. I remember her each time I see our sons who have proved to be responsible and caring. I am very proud of them, just as I was proud of their loving mother, my dearest angel.

My first son, Cephas Mandlenkosi, was born in Que Que. The tears run down my cheeks now when I see the deserted steel factories and hear the cries of workers there who have lost their jobs and are unable to look after their families. I hope and pray that before this book is published, things will have changed for the better.

Before Amaveni School opened in 1955, the main educational facility in the area was at the Globe and Phoenix mine. It was the oldest and biggest school in Que Que. The other small mines nearby ran schools which served as satellite schools. The headmaster, James Manyika, was powerful and highly respected. The establishment of Amaveni School was viewed as a challenge to Globe and Phoenix's dominance. This resulted in rivalry between the two schools in a variety of competitions, which also spilt into the local branch of the Rhodesian African Teachers Association (RATA) where I was elected as secretary but was booted out the following year because I had gone against what Globe and Phoenix teachers wanted. The problem started when I secured a bursary for a student to go to Goromonzi High School. Globe and Phoenix teachers provided me with three names as per my request but when I took their second choice, all hell broke loose. They wanted me to offer the bursary to Aleke Banda and not Boyman Mancama, who later became an executive of Anglo American Corporation in Zimbabwe. The next year, I was re-elected as branch secretary of RATA, a position I held until my transfer to Harari.

Que Que had a wide diversity of people and cultures. It reminded me of a book I had read while I was doing my Junior Certificate way back in 1948. The title of the book was *The Heart of London*, and the first sentence in the book read, "When eight million people decide to live together, things are bound to happen." This sentence depicts what society is and how we should live together and what structures we should put together to do so. The need for structures to maintain order and provide services interested me from my childhood. I always wanted to see people being organised.

I often tell people that I was a teacher by choice but a politician by circumstance. I loved teaching, but I was forced out of the profession. Let me describe what it was that really made me political. It was while I was at Dadaya Mission in 1944 as a young boy, while the Second World War was still underway and Sir Garfield Todd told us what was happening during the war, giving details of the casualties and the successes of the allied forces against Adolf Hitler.

But he also described to us the Nazi racism that had triggered the war. Sir Garfield was vehemently opposed to racism; in fact he was colour blind. He lived among the people in Shabani communal area and became part of us. When pregnant women near the mission were having problems in delivering, they called him for help, and he would go at any time of the day or night. In appreciation, the parents of the children he had helped to deliver, named their babies "Todd". Thanks to him, I grew up thinking that all men are equal, regardless of colour. But when I went into the real world, I found that things were completely different. I discovered that the colour of my skin determined what I could do and what I could not do.

In urban areas in particular, I was reminded that I was black and that I could not do so many of the ordinary things that are part of people's lives. It pained me. I hated being discriminated against because of the colour of my skin, because I was African. That is why in Que Que, for instance, I found the conditions in the African townships horrible and I felt I had to get involved and try to bring about change. I could not be a councillor because I was black, and had to be content with being on the African Advisory Board. I used to advise a white councillor who would then take our grievances to the council. When I looked at him and talked to him, I could see that he was where he was because he was white.

That put me in a fighting mood, and I felt we as Africans had to fight for our rights. From that position my approach to every organization I joined was that I had to fight in order to gain my human dignity. This discrimination occurred in the department of African education. As African teachers in a government school, we were required to undergo training under a white headmaster if we wanted to be promoted to be heads of schools; white teachers did not have to. There were schools that were headed by whites; I could not head those schools because I was black.

Headmasterships at certain schools in the Ministry of African Education were reserved for whites, like Harari High School, while Highfield High School was reserved for black headmasters. Such arrangements prevailed throughout the country. The colour of my skin was a determining factor in what I could do. The environment and the situation left me without much choice. This worried me greatly as a young person. When Garfield Todd became prime minister of what was then Southern Rhodesia, I was quite excited about it and I looked forward to some real change, but the way the whites revolted against him because they thought he was advancing Africans too quickly left me bewildered and bitter. Here was a man whom I had known to be completely colour-blind being accused of advancing the Africans too quickly. I asked myself, "Why should we not be advanced quickly? Why should our advancement be determined by white people and not ourselves?" These were the kinds of questions which worried me. I was looking for an opportunity to put them right.

It was a time of change. The British who used to boast that the sun never set on the British Empire were watching it set. India was free and so the sun was setting in the East, and was soon to begin in African countries. But this did not appear to have any effect in Rhodesia; the whites wanted to maintain the status quo, which meant that they were determined to hold their positions as

superior and to impress on the black people that we were inferior.
I could not understand. After all, during the Second World War
black people had joined the fight against Hitler. They were made
to believe that they were fighting racism and that racism should be
eliminated everywhere. But the Rhodesian whites, some of whom
fought side by side with blacks in battles against the Nazis, forgot
all that when they came back to Rhodesia.

While I was in Que Que, I was among people who felt that we
were duty bound to fight for our rights, and for our freedom and
dignity as Africans. It was a calling.

At the end of 1958 I moved to Salisbury. I travelled by train and
was met at the station by the school clerk, Pamnus Nyamurowa
(now late) who later became a popular newsreader on the African
Service of the Rhodesia Broadcasting Corporation. I was surprised
that he avoided the main road to Harari township, and later learnt
that he was driving without a valid licence and his car was not
licensed either. Such cases were very common in those days. He
took me to my house which was a stone's throw from Shingirayi
School, my new post.

As at Amaveni, the headmaster at Shingirayi was a white man,
from South Africa. I had no problem. He assigned me to run a
kindergarten school which was some distance away from the main
school and had a complement of eight teachers. My teachers and
I were happy to be on our own. I felt like a big frog in a small
pond. The township was treated like a buffer zone, between the
much bigger Highfield township and the city of Salisbury. But relations between blacks and whites were growing tense. Highfield
was becoming a no-go area for whites as it developed as the home
of African Nationalism. During outbreaks of violence, the security
forces would evacuate whites who were working in the townships.

At Shingirayi School, I introduced a savings club in 1959. The
teachers were happy to save part of their salaries from which other

teachers could borrow at an agreed interest rate. It operated for many years after I left Shingirayi, as my wife discovered when she was transferred there 20 years later.

As the year was coming to an end my headmaster received a letter of promotion. I asked him if there was anything for me mentioned in the letter. I said that if I was not promoted, it would mean the end of my teaching career. To my relief, a week later I received a letter stating that I had been promoted to be headmaster of Mhofu School in the older part of Highfield township. I was pleased to follow the footsteps of Leopold Takawira, the "bull of Chirumanzi", who had been headmaster there before me. He became vice-president of ZANU but died while in detention in Salisbury Prison in 1970.

And it was in 1959 that I had a highly embarrassing experience in Harari township. I went to a meeting of the Southern Rhodesia Football Association organisers, and after the meeting there was a lot of free beer provided for us. I over-drank. Africans had not been allowed by law to drink "European" beer until 1957. That night, I struggled to reach my house half a kilometre away. Along the way, I stumbled, fell down and lay there, asleep. One of my teachers saw me and picked me up and put me in his bed. When I was told the following morning of the state I had been in, I was so embarrassed and ashamed that I vowed never to drink again. I am still ashamed of what I did, but I am pleased that I quit drinking alcohol so that I can always be sober and accountable for my actions.

3

Life in Highfield

The year 1959 will be remembered as the one in which the Rhodesian authorities banned the African National Congress, with its slogan, "one-man, one-vote", and rounded up its leaders and detained them indefinitely and without trial. Their "crime" was to demand equal rights and the return of their land. They included some of the earliest nationalists, like James Chikerema, Daniel Madzimbamuto and Jason Moyo. Worse was to come. The white authorities were panicking and trying to stop the unstoppable. Joshua Nkomo escaped detention because he was out of the country. The British Government did nothing to stop the brutal repression of our leaders. A delegation, including Nathan Shamuyarira, the most prominent African journalist in the country, and Sir Garfield Todd, went to New York to address the United Nations on the deteriorating situation in Southern Rhodesia.

However, the ban on the ANC was ineffective, because a group of young men under the leadership of Sketchley Samkange announced the birth of the National Democratic Party on 1 January 1960, to replace the ANC. Strangely, Samkange disappeared from the political scene soon after this. I never knew why.

I was less politically active in Harari township than I had been in Amaveni, for several reasons. There was less political activity in this period because the authorities had not only banned the ANC, but had made all blacks' political meetings illegal. Not even RATA was allowed to hold meetings. Also, Harari township was much bigger and less intimate than Amaveni. One needed time to get to know people and become politically involved. Also, I had been in Harari for only one year. Despite the drastic measures taken by the minority regime, life went on.

The year 1960 saw me attain my cherished dream of being a headmaster, at Mhofu government school in Highfield. I was struck when I met my assistant teachers by the fact that that they were all older than me and had more teaching experience. I knew none of them. I had to move with caution. In addition to my youth, I was single. Both of these factors put me at a cultural disadvantage. Respect did not come easy. But I managed the school without incident. Obert, aged 15 and one of my younger brothers, was at the school as one of my pupils. He also worked for me as my cook. The two roles – teacher's brother and cook – gave him some status, which he enjoyed.

Highfield was a political melting-pot. Anything could happen at any time. It was the home of African nationalists, who were young, militant and bitter. They were reading about what was happening in the rest of Africa to the north of us. Ghana had attained independence, so had others. Malawi and Zambia were moving toward majority rule. Old Highfield, previously occupied by old residents, mostly civil servants, had adopted new names that reflected people's political aspirations – Lusaka, Canaan, Jerusalem – and showed a new diversity in culture and behaviour. Highfield was a suburb, or township, of Salisbury, and people travelled to the city centre every day to work. On buses they talked of their grievances, which were political, economic and social. It was common for friends to say, "So long life, suffer is nothing." The expression signifies a state of despair which people accepted as a way of life. It was a way of emphasising that as long as we were alive, we did not worry about the suffering we endured.

In February 1959, John Stonehouse, the British MP who later faked his death so he could run away with his mistress, addressed us and said: "You should hold your heads high and remember that this country belongs to you, the oppressed and black people of Zimbabwe." The authorities picked up his statement and deported him within 24 hours.

Activists known as "troublemakers", like James Chikerema, founder member of the ANC, George Nyandoro, member of the Salisbury Youth League, Joseph Msika, trade unionist and member of the ANC in Bulawayo, and many others, were incarcerated in Khami Prison after the banning of the ANC. But there were many others ready to step into their shoes.

The National Democratic Party (NDP) was launched in 1960 to continue with the struggle for majority rule. The message was "Forwards ever, backwards never", expressing that no amount of intimidation and repression would stop black people from reaching their goal. The NDP was more militant, more embracing and better organised than the ANC. More workers – as opposed to peasants – identified themselves with the NDP, because the new party backed trade unions, whereas the ANC had concentrated on land issues.

British Prime Minister Harold McMillan visited Africa in 1961 and made his famous speech in Cape Town, the home of the parliament for white supremacy and apartheid. His theme was the "the winds of change" sweeping across Africa and the East – the iconic warning to the white governments of southern Africa that their days were numbered.

It also fired us to redouble our efforts and to plan for armed struggle. The speech served as a warning that the British government was prepared to give independence to its former colonies and was in full support of majority rule. I decided with other teachers to reorganise the Rhodesian African Teachers' Association. Mhofu School was our venue and before long we called a meeting which was attended by the majority of teachers in Highfield. They elected me chairman of the RATA branch and I believe I made it the strongest and most powerful branch in the country. We aligned ourselves fully with the liberation movements, despite the fact that teachers were not allowed to take an active part in politics.

House 4144, Canaan, Highfield

Accommodation for teachers at the time was free. As I was single, I stayed at Canaan section, not far from Mhofu School, and shared the house with Peter Kutama, the headmaster of Mbizi School in old Highfield. Both of us were single and were of the Gumbo totem, and so were brothers. We each had our own bedroom and we shared the kitchen and dining room. We got on very well and our interests were identical except that he loved his beer. He thought that beer was not only the best drink but that it helped him forget his sorrows and problems.

One day in 1960 Robert Gabriel Mugabe joined us unannounced. He was closely related to my Gumbo brother and house-mate, Peter Kutama, and as he was on leave he had made no long -term plans for his residence. Kutama and I were bachelors, and Mugabe must have seen that he would be comfortable living with us. We quickly arranged to accommodate him at our house, 4144 in Canaan, Highfield. In those days, a visit from a friend was a source of pleasure, rather than an imposition. As he was coming from newly independent Ghana, then under Kwame Nkrumah, his arrival gave us some status. Despite the fact that we had only two bedrooms, one was given to our special guest. He seemed comfortable and it made us feel comfortable too.

Later in the year, Sally Mugabe visited us briefly from Ghana and I found her charming. We established a bond of friendship which was to continue until her death.

My relationship with Mugabe was close; he viewed me as a rel-ative, owing to my relationship with his mother Bona whose totem (Gumbo) is the same as mine. He always referred to me as "Sekuru Msipa", a sign of respect, and I called him "muzukuru", meaning "sister's child". This continued in later life, and his late siblings, remaining sister and nephews still refer to me as "sekuru" (uncle).

Mugabe was very simple in his ways and very reserved – ex-cept when discussing political issues. He always behaved correctly and was highly disciplined and focused. He looked like one of us and dressed like one of us as well – neat but not flashy. We were very open with each other and talked about anything, in addition to politics. Occasionally, my wife-to-be, Charlotte, would visit us briefly on her way to or from Monte Cassino, a Catholic girls school in Macheke, where she was training to become a home economics teacher. He told me of his own wife-to-be, Sally, who was expected soon to follow him and that she was highly political. Indeed she got involved in the women's league immediately after her arrival. As for Charlotte, he showed a great liking and respect for her.

The only favour we did was to give up a bedroom for him to have on his own. With everything else, we were equal. Obert my brother cooked sadza and vegetables at night and prepared tea with bread for breakfast. Mugabe understood our situation, as teachers with poor remuneration. He knew the conditions of black teachers in Rhodesia and so he did not expect much except ordinary African fare. He also did not appear to have made much money in Ghana. What was important was that we were happy and comfortable. Eating the same meals together brought us even closer. We had lots of time to talk of everything, about people, events and ideas.

Almost immediately Robert and I discovered our mutual passion for politics. We discussed the strategies and leadership at the time of the NDP. He supported Joshua Nkomo's continued leadership, arguing that he was the only leader with massive support throughout the country and that his removal would cause a division in the country into Mashonaland and Matebeleland. We talked about the possibility of him coming back home. He was adamant that he would not come to work under white minority rule and endure the racial discrimination which had forced him to leave for Zambia and later Ghana, the first black country to gain independence.

As chairman of RATA, I invited him to address members of our branch on life in Ghana, which we believed was a free country. It was his first public address since coming back to Rhodesia, and took place in June 1960, at Mhofu School. Reaction to that speech spread like bush fire. Soon politicians and trade unions were fighting for him to address their meetings. He was a real crowd-puller. Every weekend he was fully booked. Those who organised rallies were being asked, "Will Mugabe be speaking?"

Mugabe supported the idea of a one-party state back then, but he did not speak much about his personal experiences in Ghana. It was as if something had gone wrong while he was in Ghana, which he did not disclose.

One sunny day in 1960 Enos Nkala and Moton Malianga visited me and asked if they could speak to Mugabe. This was just a formality; they did not have to ask for entrance into my home. Nkala was a vibrant politician who was opposed to Nkomo's leadership of the movement. They came in, and within 30 minutes a deal had been sealed. Mugabe was to send his resignation to Ghana and would accept the position of secretary for information and publicity in the NDP. This meant that he would leave his well-paid teaching job in order to work for the liberation of his homeland for no pay. It was a big sacrifice for him.

Officials of the National Democratic Party after Nkomo's return to Southern Rhodesia, November 1960 (l to r: J.Z. Moyo, M. Malianga, J. Nkomo, E. Nkala, R.G. Mugabe)

But in those days we reminded ourselves of "the three S's" in the struggle – suffering, sacrifice and service. Mugabe in 1960 in my house undertook to suffer, sacrifice and serve. It was a momentous decision and I was delighted. I congratulated him heartily.

He took his new job seriously and zealously. His appointment heralded a new revolutionary approach to our politics. Every morning he woke up and boarded the bus to work. He did not finish at 5 p.m. like others, but remained in the NDP offices in Salisbury's Railway Avenue after working hours to allow members to present their reports to him. His dedication and commitment inspired our members. The Special Branch police kept a close watch on him. For the first time, they found themselves dealing with somebody who was not only highly educated but extremely intelligent and eloquent. He was entered on their list of "dangerous Africans" who had to be closely monitored and, preferably, arrested.

Occasionally, he had moments of relaxation. It was during one of these rare occasions that we took some friends for lunch at Mtanga Restaurant at Machipisa shopping centre in HIghfield. We could not eat in Salisbury's city centre because of the colour bar in restaurants. The four of us agreed to have something on the menu called "goulash". We waited with keen interest to see what the goulash would be. It turned out to be sadza. Mugabe angrily asked the waiter what it was he was serving. He replied, "It is sadza". Mugabe ordered him to take it back and write sadza on the menu. The waiter's explanation was that having "goulash" on the menu attracted customers. We were not impressed and we had to go over the menu again to choose what we wanted to eat. Imagine, people were being tricked into choosing from meaningless foreign names. Mugabe was not amused.

I also got to know him as a caring friend. One Friday afternoon I bought a car, a blue Zephyr. They were all the rage then. Not only did I not have a driver's licence but I didn't know how to drive. The following day, Mugabe was shocked when he came home at lunch to hear that I had driven to Harari Hospital, alone. He immediately boarded a bus to follow me there. I was standing and talking to a nurse under the shade of a big tree. He was extremely angry and shouted, "Why do you do this? See the anxiety you caused me!" He did not even greet the young woman. I asked him to give me time to finish my conversation. But he demanded that I give him the car keys. I was annoyed, and to avoid further embarrassment I handed the keys to him and told him to leave us alone. I remember that occasion because it was the only time he took an order from me.

In those days, state registered nurses earned more than teachers and looked down on us, calling us "pedestrians" who couldn't afford their own transport. I had driven to Harari Hospital to show them that I had graduated from being a pedestrian to being an owner of a car. After I returned to the car, Mugabe drove us back home. He had a driver's licence and owned a car himself in Ghana, which was later shipped to Zimbabwe. He nagged me all the way for what I had done. He was treating me like a school teacher talking to a naughty school boy. He just stopped short of smacking me! But it showed he cared about my safety, like a sincere friend.

Mugabe was becoming bitter with the intractable political situation, and was looking for action to demonstrate to the Rhodesian authorities that we meant business. In the evening of 20 July, 1960, at an NDP meeting at Cyril Jennings Hall in Highfield, he called on the people to march on Salisbury's city centre. Like people possessed, we marched that night in our thousands from Highfield.

When we got to Harari township, we found the police armed to the teeth. They had guns, batons and vicious dogs. We backed off and regrouped at Stodart Hall in the township where Mugabe addressed the crowd almost continuously for two days, stopping only for a few minutes for rest or refreshment. People would go to work and come back to listen to him. I was there the first day up to 4 a.m. but then had to leave to teach at school.

Highfield was becoming ungovernable. A state of emergency had been declared and Highfield was placed under curfew, giving law enforcement agencies licence to deal with violators ruthlessly. Everyone entering or leaving the township was searched as the police tried to screen for rabble-rousers. Boniface Gumbo, a party activist, heard that he was on the wanted list, and begged me and Peter Kutama to get him out one night. We agreed to put him in the boot of my car and to drive through a roadblock, knowing very well that if the police found him we would be in very serious trouble. Fortunately, we were allowed to pass through after having to answer a few questions. Gumbo escaped and we thanked our ancestral spirits. I will never forget that incident. But I know that thousands of our young people went through much more dangerous situations later, and took far greater risks in their quest for a free Zimbabwe.

However, as the NDP grew increasingly powerful the authorities were becoming more extreme in their repression. The NDP was banned hardly a year after its formation, just as the ANC had been in 1959.

We began to ask ourselves, was it necessary to continue forming political parties which would be banned? Why was Joshua Nkomo always out of the country when the bannings took place? Should we not operate underground and resort to guerrilla tactics?

After considerable discussion, we resolved that despite the possibility of banning orders, we would form a successor party that would not only replace the NDP but would also plan to execute the armed struggle. The Zimbabwe African People's Union (ZAPU) was formed on 17 December, 1961. Like the NDP, it was militant and dedicated to the national liberation of Rhodesia. Joshua Nkomo was elected as president, Dr Samuel Parirenyatwa as vice-president, Ndabaningi Sithole, who was president of RATA, as chairman, Jason Moyo, a trade unionist and former executive member of the ANC, as secretary general, Robert Mugabe as information and publicity secretary, Leopold Takawira as secretary for external affairs and Joseph Msika, former trade unionist and member of the previously banned ANC executive, as a committee member. The coming on board of Dr Parirenyatwa, the first African doctor in Rhodesia, was a cause for celebration throughout the country. It was a big challenge to other African professionals to follow suit. Unfortunately he was killed in a car crash on the Gwelo-Bulawayo road under controversial circumstances while on party duty on 14 August, 1962.

Scarcely a year after its formation, ZAPU too was banned and, as had become routine, its leaders were arrested and many of them banished to remote rural areas. Frustration was also building up within the leadership. Disappointment was turning into discontent. The question of whether to form another party took centre stage again.

The result was a split in the nationalist movement and the formation of ZANU, the Zimbabwe African National Union, in August 1963. This split was to dominate the country's politics for more than 20 years.

One of the biggest factors which led to the split was Nkomo's leadership. He had been president successively of the ANC, the NDP and ZAPU between 1957 and 1963. Naturally people were now impatient with the failure to attain majority rule, and Nkomo became the scapegoat. They thought he was not militant enough, and accused him of being a moderate. He had also been spending a great deal of time outside Zimbabwe, trying to draw attention to the country's politics and raising support from friendly countries and organisations.

His critics accused him of deliberately being out of the country to avoid being detained with the other leaders. There were some in the movement, such as Enos Nkala, who had a pathological hatred of Nkomo. It was no surprise that the formation of ZANU took place in his house in Highfield.

There was also Reverend Ndabaningi Sithole, who appeared to be driven to become a leader, of anything, anyhow. When he was a teacher at Dadaya, he organised a strike in the hope of taking over control from Sir Garfield Todd. It failed. At a meeting of RATA in August 1959, where he had been invited to speak as a guest of honour, he ended up challenging its president, G.D Mhlanga, for the leadership. A few of the teachers queried the fact that he was not a delegate and was not qualified to stand for office, but he was a gifted orator and somehow he got himself elected as president.

To start with, Nkomo tried to avoid policies that endorsed violence, but it was taken by others as weakness.

ZANU was formed on 8 August, 1963, at the meeting in Nkala's house, when Ndabaningi Sithole, backed by Henry Hamadziripi, former member of the ANC, NDP and ZAPU, Mukudzei Midzi, a former school clerk, Hebert Chitepo, the first African lawyer in Southern Rhodesia, Edgar Tekere, trade unionist, and Leopold Takawira, former headmaster who had resigned to enter politics, decided to split from ZAPU. When it became known that Robert Mugabe had joined them, Joshua Nkomo was shattered, and expressed his shock and dismay.

The split was followed by the worst violence ever witnessed in the country since the turn of the century. Throughout 1963 and 1964 Zimbabweans were involved in a war of self-destruction. Pangas, bricks, stones and petrol bombs were used against each other. Mufakose and Highfield were the worst affected. I knew families whose houses were either demolished or petrol bombed.

My house was stoned, and on one occasion a big rock landed on the pillow of my two-and-a-half-year-old son, Cephas Mandlenkosi, missing his head by half an inch. Wardrobes were placed next to windows to prevent missiles hitting people inside their homes. Many fled to quieter townships in fear of their lives. Eddison Zvobgo, the American-trained lawyer and ZANU official, had his house destroyed in Mufakose. There are still people with scars as a result of the petrol bombing. The government declared a state of emergency to try to control the violence, but also used it as pretext to take action against ZAPU and ban ZANU. The leaders were rounded up and detained in remote areas – ZAPU officials and supporters were held at Gonakudzingwa in the south-east border area, and those from ZANU at Sikhombela in the Gokwe area, and Wha Wha in the Midlands. The detentions were effected under the notorious Law and Order Maintenance Act which provided for detention without trial, and were continued long after 1964.

With almost the entire leadership of the African nationalist movement removed from society, Prime Minister Ian Smith felt confident to make a Unilateral Declaration of Independence (UDI) on the 11 November, 1965, without fear of causing an uprising. Following UDI, more arrests were made and I was among the victims, being incarcerated from November 1965 to December 1970.

When the split occurred, Mugabe had approached me and asked if I would join ZANU. I told him I would not, because I did not trust Ndabaningi Sithole. He then said to me, "I hope this will not affect our relationship."

"Why should it?" I replied, and indeed it in no way affected our friendship, which continues up to now. He remains my "Muzukuru" and I remain his "Sekuru".

In 1981, when Robert Mugabe had become prime minister of Zimbabwe, following our independence in1980, he included me in his delegation to the Organisation of African Union conference which was held in Nairobi. As we were having dinner, he reminded me of our discussion in 1963 concerning the question, whether I would join ZANU.

"Do you still remember what you said then?"

"I remember it very well."

"What did you say?"

"I told you that I was not going to join you because I did not trust Sithole."

He and Maurice Nyagumbo, who was with him, laughed. He then came to the gist of the matter.

"Now that I am your 'Muzukuru' and the president of ZANU(PF), do you also not trust me?"

I smiled the kind of smile which gives one time to think.

"May I ask you a question before I answer yours?"

"Go ahead."

"If I answer you in a manner you don't like, are you not likely to leave me in Nairobi?"

They burst into laughter and Mugabe said we should agree not to pursue the subject. So I got off the hook.

When I was safely back in Harari, he called me to continue from where we had left off. I was now free to state my views. I said, "You know if I joined ZANU(PF), my friends in PF ZAPU will condemn me as a sellout and those in ZANU(PF) will describe me as an opportunist. Because I don't want those labels, I cannot join you, though I have nothing against you. What you need is to get Joshua Nkomo on your side, not for defections from PF ZAPU to ZANU(PF)." I got the impression that he took note of what I had said.

Nearly 25 years after this conversation, I was the happiest man when Nkomo and Mugabe agreed to work together under the Unity Accord of 1987. It was to me a dream come true.

Despite the upheavals in Highfield in 1960, people carried on with their lives, and got married – Charlotte and I among them – and children were born. The politically active were prepared to suffer and sacrifice for their cause, even if it meant incarceration or death. It was the beginning of the armed struggle. The NDP, ZAPU and ZANU had been declared illegal organisations and had been banned, but it did not affect the commitment and desire of the people for freedom.

A big change in my life had come in 1960. That is when I tied the knot with Sithabile Charlotte Matabela at St Martin's Anglican Church in Amaveni township in Que Que. She had waited for me from 1955 when I told her that I loved her and was going to marry her. In between times some people were telling her that she was wasting her time but she believed in me and loved me, until 27 April, 2013 when she suddenly departed from this world. I remember the things we did together, her amazing patience and love and above all our wonderful sons she left behind to care for and comfort me.

***

Around the time that Mugabe moved into my house in Highfield, and the political atmosphere was being ratcheted up, my professional life continued. At the end of 1960, I received a letter from the Ministry of Education appointing me headmaster of Crowborough No.1 School in Mufakose township. It went further to instruct me to take up my new post as soon as schools closed. I had heard that a new township, Mufakose, was being established and two schools, Crowborough 1 and 2, had been built there. Because these new schools were larger than the ones in Highfield, and being the youngest and most junior of the headmasters in that township, I assumed my seniors would receive the headships, so I had taken no interest in what was happening in Mufakose. My appointment was a very pleasant surprise to me but a shock to my seniors. Nobody congratulated me, even though I was the secretary of the Headmasters' Association. The reason why they wanted me to go early was that they wanted me to enrol the pupils for both schools. The headmaster for No. 2 had not been appointed. Herbert Ramashu from Bulawayo came to take up his position in January 1961 and I had the pleasure of handing over a list of his pupils to him. The Ramushus became close family friends.

Mufakose, which was previously open land known as Crow-borough Farm, was built mainly for workers from the industrial areas of Salisbury. Most had young families, and they included salesman, public relations assistants, clerks, drivers, semi-skilled workers and manual labourers. At my school, which we named Tendayi, the teachers were young, and mostly from the first group of graduates from a new Teachers' Training College in Umtali. You could see the excitement on their faces and their eagerness to put into practice what they had learnt at college. They were all raring to go. Instead of managing eight teachers as was the case at Mhofu, I now had 36! One of the older teachers there was David Ndoda who had taught me at Dadaya Primary School. He was the most supportive and co-operative of the whole lot, which says some-thing about Dadaya. Some of my students whose progress and development I still follow with pride include George Chiweshe, a judge in the High Court, Phineas Chiota, a businessman and Web-ster Shamu, a journalist. Both the latter are also members of par-liament. Each time I attend weddings and other gatherings, partic-ularly in Harare, I am humbled when my former pupils, some of them now grandmothers, greet me and remind me of our days at Tendayi. The school included teachers' accommodation which at the time was spacious compared to what were used to.

Charlotte joined me in Mufakose. That was the beginning of my family life. I had to learn quickly how to live with her. I had to report to her where I was going when I went out, and had to give a reason when I came home late. It was beautiful that both of us were looking forward to living together when we made our vows in the church before so many people. When she was due to deliver our first baby, I took her to Que Que to be with her parents who, according to our culture, were to take full responsibility for the safe delivery of her baby. On 18 March, 1961, I was excited to hear that God had blessed us with a bouncing baby boy. I named him Cephas, and gave him Mandlenkosi as his second name, after his maternal grandfather. This brought great joy to the Msipa and Matabela families. There is no other place now which I identify with more than Mufakose. My four sons, Cephas, Christopher, Charles and Elijah, were all born and grew up in Mufakose. No wonder that at my wife's funeral, buses full of people from Mufakose came to mourn her passing.

Mufakose lay next to Highfield, and the residents faced similar problems, if not worse because they were farther away from their place of work, which meant that they paid more for transport. The political environment was the same.

It was also the year that ZAPU was formed and people's involvement and interest in politics in Mufakose was as intense as it was in Highfield. As one of the earliest residents in the township and its first headmaster, my political support was automatic and enthusiastic. I became more active and involved than I had been in Highfield, and had no serious competitors. In time, my political influence seemed to be felt particularly among the youth, many of whom had passed through my school. I was a well-known ZAPU leader, even though I had no official title after my name.

After the split in the nationalist movement, I made sure that ZANU's membership in Mufakose was kept to a minimum. Mistrust grew between me and my former friends who had transferred their allegiance to ZANU, and a clash was inevitable. I recruited ZAPU youths to guard my house against attack. The result of this was that I was charged by police for having illegal "bodyguards". But in the magistrate's court, the state failed to prove the case against me and I was acquitted.

All in all I was closely connected with nationalist politics in Mufakose. My dismissal from teaching later was when I was a headmaster in Mufakose. My subsequent arrest and detention were carried out in Mufakose. Everyone in Mufakose followed closely what I and my family went through in our desire to free Zimbabwe from colonialism and minority rule. I was able to resume my activities in the Rhodesian African Teachers' Association when the teachers of the two schools in Mufakose formed a branch of RATA and elected me as their chairperson.

My subsequent election as national president of RATA made me the pride of Mufakose and enhanced my status socially and politically. Each time I visit Mufakose, I feel like I am visiting my home. I have a wonderful feeling for Mufakose.

It was in this capacity that I went to the 1961 RATA annual conference, which was held at Fletcher High School in Gwelo, and led a delegation of teachers from Mufakose. We expected to discuss salaries and conditions of service. But most of the RATA leaders there – including secretary-general Peter Mahlangu and national treasurer Elliott Dhula – were university graduates, while the majority of the teachers had not gone further than high school. There was a strong feeling among the teachers that the graduates did not understand the grievances of non-graduates and were not the right people to speak on their behalf. This feeling had been rumbling for several years and yet, when elections came round, the graduates were elected overwhelmingly. There were teachers amongst us – but I was not one of them – who felt that the only way to remove the graduates was to give them no chance to address teachers or to defend themselves. This was because they believed that delegates from the rural areas would be swayed by the graduates' fluency in English and vote them back into office. A group of mostly urban teachers devised a plan. As soon as the meeting was called to order, there was a resolution calling for elections to be held before other business. The leadership was taken by surprise, but ended up giving in to the demand.

The vote was held and it resulted in an effective coup d'état. The old order had changed and yielded to a new executive. Those who had been invited to address the conference – including Sir Garfield Todd, as the former prime minister of Southern Rhodesia – were surprised when they were welcomed by new faces. They were more shocked when they were told what had happened. A reporter from the *Daily News*, the main African-read newspaper in the country, wrote, "I saw a sin being committed and I witnessed the Doom of RATA." Caleb Somkence, a teacher from Bulawayo, was president, and I became vice-president.

Before the end of the year, Somkence was appointed to represent the Federal Government in Lagos, so I took over the presidency in accordance with the RATA constitution. I was re-elected thereafter until December 1964. It was then that I had called a special meeting of the executive of the association.

I had invited the permanent secretary in the Ministry of African Education, A.J. Smith, to address teachers. The conference was at Ranche House College in Salisbury; halfway through his speech he was called to attend to an urgent telephone call from Phillip Smith, then the Minister of Education. I remember it as if was yesterday what A.J. Smith told us when he returned from taking his call: "Teachers, I have bad news for you. I have been told by my minister to tell you that your president has been dismissed from teaching and he will not be allowed to teach again as long as the Rhodesian Front is in power."

I was aghast. I said, "You mean me?" and he said, "Yes."

"Is this how you dismiss your teachers?"

He explained that in my case he thought he should tell the teachers who elected me that my dimissal had nothing to do with my teaching, but with my political activities as president of RATA.

I told him, "I was fighting the Rhodesian Front privately but now I am going to fight it publicly. To get back into teaching, I have a responsibility to see that the RF goes, and the sooner the better."

He expected me to apologise, but I was confident that the RF was on its way out and that majority rule would come.

My reply did not impress some of the teachers, and after Smith left the meeting, my dismissal became the main topic of the conference.

Before he left the meeting, Smith had said, to placate the teachers, that the government was prepared to pay a secretary-general chosen by RATA the same salary that was paid to headmaster Msipa. A heated debate ensued, and it ended with me being elected as secretary-general, irrespective of the government's termination of my teaching job. Heyi James Malaba took over as RATA president. As a headmaster, my house was in the school premises and it was embarrassing to remain there for eight months when I was no longer in the job.

The government paid my salary as secretary-general of RATA for only one month; after that, fortunately, the World Organisation of the Teaching Profession (WOTP) took over and paid me from February to November 1965.

During my time as president of RATA, I addressed several meetings around the country, and was often treated almost like a head of state. Teachers admired what they said was my bravery and candidness in confronting those in authority. RATA had evolved into a wing of the nationalist movement. Internationally, I put the organisation on the map through establishing relationships with the World Confederation of Teachers' Unions (WCTU) in New York, and I attended the 1963 annual conference in Rio de Janeiro. We organised scholarships for teachers from each province to go to Canada under the sponsorship of the Canadian Teachers' Association. Regrettably, some of them never came back home after completing their training, nor did they bother to communicate with RATA.

I clashed with the authorities repeatedly. The worst occasion was in 1963 at Fletcher High School, when members of RATA ordered me not to allow C.S. Davis, the permanent secretary, to speak unless he was going to announce new salary scales for teachers. He was the guest of honour, and immediately after I had introduced him, I asked him if he was going to tell us about new salary scales. He said very emphatically that he was not. I said, in that case I would not allow him to address the teachers. This was in the glare of the press and you can imagine how embarrassed and humiliated he felt as he packed his briefcase to leave the conference hall. He went to the house of the principal, a Mr Winter. They decided to hit back. Davis called me and asked me if I was aware that all schools were under his control. I said, "Yes, I am aware." He then asked, "Between you and me, who has the right to chase the other?" He went on to ask me to tell the teachers to leave within 30 minutes or he would order us off the school premises. I was forced to plead with him and to assure him that he was free to address the teachers, even if he would not talk about salaries. I returned to the meeting to persuade the teachers to allow Mr Davis to address them. A small minority wanted the meeting called off but the majority heeded my plea. We were humbled. Davis came back to address the teachers and our meeting proceeded as if nothing had happened. It was front page news in the papers the next day – Msipa ordering the permanent secretary out of a RATA meeting. The Rhodesian Front was not amused. And it was looking for every opportunity to get at me.

The split in the nationalist movement was affecting the smooth running of the association. My secretary for publicity was Agrey Mutambanengwe and he was ZANU. He tried everything possible to get teachers to pass a vote of no confidence in me. I ignored him and teachers forgot about him. I made it clear that outside RATA, teachers were free to belong to ZAPU or ZANU but inside RATA, we were one. The teachers accepted this stance. We remained as one during my term of office as president and as secretary-general.

Caleb Somkence's term of office as RATA's president was the shortest ever, from August to December 1961, when he had to take up a post for the federal government in Nigeria. On taking over I was determined to show the union and the country that real change could be achieved. We started by reviewing the country's policy on education. We declared that we were in favouor of equal educational opportunity for every child regardless of race, colour or creed. The Rhodesian educational authorities described this as "communist propaganda".

In December of 1961, while my wife and I were driving Caleb Somkence to the railway station in Lochinvar, we were stopped by police reservists at a roadblock in the centre of the whites-only suburb around the station. They wanted to know why we were driving through a European residential area

I asked how I could get to the station without passing through the so-called European suburb. Instead of answering me, one of the white policemen hit me with a baton, aiming for my head but hitting my arm as I tried to protect myself. He ordered me out of the area immediately. I felt humiliated and bitter, but I realised that this kind of treatment was meted out to black people all the time and that was why we had fight to regain human dignity and our rights.

Most of our problems then had to do with racial discrimination. There were two distinct ministries of education – one African and the other for white schools. White children received a flying start in comparison to African children. African women teachers were given a raw deal in terms of pay and promotion opportunities. Some African schools had headships reserved for whites, which were conveniently situated in urban areas, while black teachers were usually appointed to schools a long way from the cities. The budget for African schools was less than one twentieth of that for

white schools. Church-run mission schools in rural areas carried
a far greater burden of African education than the government.

These and other issues occupied me most of the time. RATA
grew stronger and stronger and proved wrong those who predicted its doom. In January 1965, I opened an office in Harare.

4

Life in Detention

Soon after UDI in November 1965, I was called by a deputy commissioner of the British South Africa Police[1] who, after asking me about my association with Rhodesian nationalists operating in Zambia, openly asked me to be an informer. I had not been to Zambia, and my only contact with the party in exile there was through James Chikerema, Nkomo's deputy, who phoned me from time to time. I was incensed. I could not hide my anger. I told him that I felt greatly insulted to be asked to do such a thing. He also became angry and started threatening me with detention and warning me of what would happen to my family. He said they would have no one to look after them. My reply was that if birds can survive why shouldn't my family? If I cared for my family I had better think again, he said. I replied that he was free to do what he wanted. He ended by giving me ten days in which to respond to his offer. Our discussion ended on a hostile note after an hour.

I thought his remarks were an idle threat until members of

---

1   As the Rhodesian Police were known at the time.

the Special Branch entered my office at around 10.30 a.m. on 17 December, 1965, only two days after the encounter with a search warrant and a detention order. On my detention order was written, "You are likely to engage in subversive activities."

After going through all the papers they could lay their hands on, they drove me to my house in Mufakose and searched there again. I was deeply worried that what freedom I had was being taken away from me by the stroke of a pen. I would be forced to leave my wife and children to fend for themselves.

I was put into a cell at Salisbury Central Police Station. My bed was a bare plank and I was alone for 48 hours. After three days, the station's officer-in-charge – he was not Rhodesian but British – sent for me from my cell and said he was going to release me. He said that it would be illegal to hold me for more than 48 hours, and he refused to break the law. It was a Sunday, and the Special Branch panicked and tried to persuade him to keep me locked up until Monday. But the officer-in-charge was adamant. "The law is the law", he said.

So Special Branch released me briefly, and then, when the senior officer's back was turned, they re-arrested me and took me to Matapi police station in Harari township.

I experienced hell on earth that night. I did not sleep a wink. The cell was overcrowded and filthy and stinking. People were shoved in like bags of maize. Most of them were drunk and some of them were vomiting. The police could not care less. One night at Matapi was like a week at Salisbury Central. It was torture. I kept asking myself, "Do these people know that we are human beings? Why treat us like pigs?" How relieved I was to get out alive. I was transferred back to Salisbury Central.

***

I spent that Christmas and New Year in Salisbury Central prison. There were many others in there, awaiting transfer to Gonakudzingwa restriction camp, in the far south-east of the country, close to the Mozambican frontier town of Vila Salazar, where the railway line crossed into Mozambique. We were kept with prisoners on remand who were awaiting their court appearances. They held meetings in the prison courtyard in which the veteran prisoners were teaching the new arrivals how to defend themselves in court. They called it the "law school", and they held court sessions and mock trials every morning.

After about six weeks we were told that a plane was ready to take us to Gonakudzingwa. Once we had boarded we were hand-cuffed. I asked myself where they thought we could escape to and what would happen if the plane crashed. But we arrived there without incident.

We were taken to Camp No. 6, the last of six, built like an army barracks, heavily guarded and surrounded by barbed wire. We were welcomed warmly by the restrictees and shown our sleeping quarters where we were held in groups of eight. In our group was Chief Wedza from Shabani who was the oldest in the camp. He must have been over 70 years old. Why they found it necessary to restrict such an old man, I could not understand. We took turns to cook on an open fire. We fetched firewood for ourselves and we were given pots and plates. Fortunately, the people in my group understood my position as a former headmaster. Making fire was a big problem for me and I was a terrible cook. They took over when it was my turn. It was very kind of them.

I soon learnt the difference between restriction and detention. In restriction, conditions are less rigorous. At Gonakudzingwa, people were initially allowed to go outside the fence to fetch fire-wood, but eventually security was tightened. The camp was very isolated and it was easy to slip into the bush. Morale amongst us was high and people believed that freedom would somehow come soon and all that we needed was patience and commitment. So they were content to stay there for what they believed would be a short while. When some of them heard that I was planning to escape, they said that Nkomo, who was also under restriction there, had insisted on maintaining discipline and ordered us to remain in the camps.

Joshua Nkomo (centre with radio) and other inmates at Gonakudzingwa in 1964

In the meantime, the British Government was blowing hot and cold. The Labour Party under Harold Wilson was in power and was convinced that sanctions would bring the Rhodesian government down. Wilson made the fatal mistake of declaring that no British troops would be sent to Rhodesia to fight "our kith and kin". With this public statement, we began to realise that we should not expect much from the British as long as those in power in Rhodesia were largely of British descent. The comprehensive economic sanctions imposed by the United Nations looked comprehensively inescapable but the Rhodesian government and its businessmen evaded them. Smith remained in power for another 15 years.

In Salisbury, Stella Madzimbamuto, a senior nursing sister at Harare Hospital, had been fighting in the courts for the release of her husband, Daniel, who was detained at Gwelo Prison. Daniel was ZAPU and one of the first detainees in 1959. Her case, *Madzimbamuto v Lardner-Burke,* in the Supreme Court in Salisbury, proved to be probably the most important legal case in Rhodesian history, as she challenged the legality of the Law and Order (Maintenance) Act, and, at the heart of the problem, the existence of the Rhodesian independence constitution. The Appellate Division of the High Court finally ruled in 1968 that the Smith government was the *de facto* government of Rhodesia, but it withheld *de jure* recognition.

***

Didymus Mutasa – who was working with Guy and Molly Clutton-Brock, a liberal British couple who ran the multiracial Cold Comfort Farm Co-operative outside Salisbury, and gave shelter and relief to politicians and others – contacted some of us and urged us to come to Salisbury and challenge the Rhodesian government in court. We were allowed visitors and they carried messages back and forth for us. The British Government had declared that any act of the Salisbury government committed after 11 November, 1965 – the date of UDI – was unlawful. Many of us had been arrested after 11 November, so our detention was illegal. Back in Gonakudzingwa, I – who was the oldest in our group – and fellow restrictees Byron Hove, Herbert Musikavanhu, and Shakespeare Makoni from the University of Rhodesia – agreed to take up the challenge. We planned to break out between 7 p.m. and 10 p.m. For the next two weeks we studied the movements of police guards in those three hours. We discussed with the party youths detained with us how to exit from the camp. They helped us to escape by lifting the barbed wire.

Everything went according to plan, including the Mozambican guide, arranged for us by Mutasa, who was to take us to Malipati,a a small town near Chiredzi that would give us access to transport that we hoped would ultimately take us back to Salisbury. One evening in March 1966 we sneaked out of the camp, following our guide. To get from Gonakudzingwa to Malipati, we had to walk about 30 kilometres, mostly through Gonarezhou National Park, with its large populations of lion, elephant, rhino and buffalo.

We covered most of the journey at night using footpaths. It turned out to be the longest journey I have ever undertaken on foot. In the middle of the night we stopped in a field we were passing through and helped ourselves to watermelons from someone's crop. We were hungry and exhausted. Our guide assured us that it was not a crime to eat as much watermelon as we could, provided we took nothing for sale. He seemed to understand the culture of the local Shangaan people. We were very hungry and we needed the energy to continue with our long journey. It was dark, but this did not bother our guide. He did not tell us we were passing through a game reserve with dangerous animals for fear we would be frightened and want to turn back. But the ancestral spirits were with us and we travelled through the National Park safely. When we got to Malipati, one of the first questions the people asked us was how we travelled uharmed through the game park. Our honest answer was that we did not know that it was one until we came across some elephant dung.

After sunrise, Shakespeare Makoni began to get cold feet. He said it would demoralise his wife whom he was expecting to visit him shortly if she found he had escaped and left no word. Byron Hove[2] quickly and emphatically told him that there was no going back and that he could consider himself under arrest from that moment onwards. We would henceforth keep all his movements under surveillance.

The march continued and we got to Malipati shopping centre at around 1 p.m. Our guide bade us farewell and went back to Mo-

---

2 Subsequently, Byron Hove accepted an offer to travel to the UK for legal training. He became a barrister.

zambique. He was a first-class gentleman who knew the route between Gonakudzingwa and Malipati like the back of his hand. He had led us for nearly 20 hours and never faltered. He was special in every respect and he deserved to be thanked in a special way.

Nothing went well for us in Malipati. The people were most unfriendly to strangers. Communication was a big problem. They did not speak Shona and we did not understand Shangani. But we managed to find out that there was no reliable or regular transport between Malipati and Chiredzi, the nearest major town from where we were – a distance of about 200 kilometres. Our only hope was the government transport which brought health ministry people to spray malarial mosquitoes in the area. We waited and prayed for this to happen. For three nights we slept on cardboard boxes. Our jackets were our blankets at night. It was tough but we reminded ourselves that our freedom fighters were facing tougher times than we were. Then on the fourth morning we heard the sound of a Land Rover. Our reaction was mixed. We were fugitives who were being hunted high and low, but we had no alternative other than to take a chance and ask for a lift to Chiredzi town. We introduced ourselves as teachers from Zimuto School in Victoria Province and said we had visited some friends in Malipati but our car had broken down. Whether they believed us or not, I don't know, but they agreed to give the four of us a lift, free of charge. What a gamble it was, but what a relief it turned out to be. We knew that the police were looking for us and had erected road blocks on all major roads. By travelling in a government vehicle we feared we would be handing ourselves over to the police. But what was the alternative? To wait in Malipati? To walk all the way to Chiredzi?

God smiled on us and we arrived safely in Chiredzi. There were only a few roadblocks and they allowed us to pass. The last thing they would have expected would have been to find us in an official vehicle. We smiled as our driver was ordered to pass through the town. After being dropped off, we were warned by a police patrol not to enter Chiredzi's township as they did not want strangers there. We repeated our story to the senior officer, a young white man, that we wanted to get transport to Zimuto School further along the main road to Fort Victoria . A big petrol tanker stopped by that evening and offered a lift, but said he could take only one of us. Makoni jumped at the offer and the rest of us spent the night on the veranda of the shop. We heard later that Makoni was arrested at a roadblock in Mvuma. We finally got to Salisbury after evading the police at night by taxi and we found Didymus Mutasa waiting for us at Cold Comfort Farm, about ten kilometres outside Salisbury. He and his welcoming party greeted us and said, "We have been told that the judges cannot stop the police from arresting you for escaping from detention. Their function is to hear your case when the police bring you for trial. We have two offers to make to you. The first is for you to leave for Zambia via Botswana tonight with our assistance. The second is to go underground with the clear knowledge that you will be arrested and that you will have the opportunity to challenge the legality of your arrest and detention which is illegal according to the British Government."

I told him that as far as I was concerned, I had no choice but to stick to what I had come back to Salisbury for, and that was to challenge the legality of my arrest and detention, whatever the consequences might be. I moved to Cold Comfort and settled in with Mutasa, Moven Mahachi and Patrick Chinamasa, all of whom became senior ministers in Mugabe's government after independence. The farm was under constant police surveillance and yet it took ten weeks for the police to discover my hideout and to arrest me.

I enjoyed my stay at Cold Comfort Farm. We shared the little we had and worked in our fields. Special Branch detectives came to see Mutasa from time to time to enquire about me. I saw them but they did not recognise me because I was dressed in overalls and looked like an ordinary labourer, either looking after sheep or irrigating vegetables. My wife and children and friends came to visit me. I wrote letters to friends but I was careful to have them posted in Bulawayo. I knew that one day I would be arrested and would have the opportunity to demonstrate to the world that Smith would ignore the Rhodesian judiciary if the court ruled in my favour.

Eventually I was arrested at Cold Comfort. Special Branch security details came one night in May 1966. They must have been following the people who came to see me, because they knew exactly where I was sleeping. I was taken to Fort Victoria where I was presented in the magistrate's court. The lawyer, Labas Cagney from the firm of Scanlen & Holderness, came from Salisbury to defend me. He argued that Smith's government, after the UDI on 11 November, was illegal and, since I was arrested on 17 November, I had no case to answer. Walter Kamba,[3] the lawyer who was supposed to represent me, had escaped arrest himself two days before my trial. To my pleasant surprise the magistrate agreed with my lawyer. Unfortunately there was no press coverage of the hearing, so no one except my friends got to know that I was victorious in court.

Despite my acquittal, however, I was served with a detention order soon after. I was taken to Fort Victoria and my detention in the Remand Prison there was one of the worst experiences in my life. I fell ill with appendicitis and the prison medical officer ordered that I be sent to Fort Victoria General Hospital for an operation.

The surgery went well. But as I was being wheeled to my hospital bed, I saw that I had leg irons around my ankles. I could not

---

3   Later Vice Chancellor of the University of Zimbabwe.

believe it. Did they really think I was going to run away immediately after the operation? The nurses protested to the two prison guards who answered that they were carrying out instructions
from the prison superintendent, and their duty was to carry them
out to the letter. I became a great attraction and the source of rumours in the hospital. Some thought I was a murderer and others
that I was a robber. Eventually the truth came out that I was a political detainee and I became a big hero. Patients wanted to know
about the political struggle and how life was at Gonakudzingwa.
I enjoyed being the centre of attention, but it was painful to have
the shackles around my ankles day and night. At night I had to
roll a towel around my ankles to stop the metal from cutting into
my flesh.

Another incident angered me while I was in hospital. My wife
and my sister, Sihlaleleni Mpofu, heard that I had undergone surgery and they drove all the way from Salisbury to Fort Victoria to
see me. They were not allowed into the hospital. Instead, I was
told by prison guards to sit up so that they could see me from
outside through the window, which was some distance away from
me. I had to use sign language to communicate with them. As a
remand prisoner, I was not allowed to speak to them without the
authority of the prison authorities. The guards could have advised
my wife and sister to apply to the local prison authorities for permission to see me. It was a complete waste of time for them and
deeply frustrating.

After a week in hospital, arrangements were made for me to
be handed over to the police who were to take me back to Gwelo
Prison. Indeed, the Special Branch officer was awaiting this duty
with pleasure. It was almost impossible to escape from the prison in Gwelo. It had been used to detain high-profile figures such
as Dr Hastings Kamuzu Banda[4] before he became president of

---

4 Following the declaration of a state of emergency in Nyasaland, Hastings Banda, along with hundreds of other Africans, was arrested on 3 March

Malawi. (He unfortunately became a dictator who had himself declared "President for Life" and as a result ended up a miserable and most hated man.)

I was taken to the prison at night and the following day I was pleased to see so many friends, including Willie Musarurwa and Boniface Gumbo. The Gwelo Prison was reserved for my party, PF ZAPU, while Salisbury Prison took in ZANU leaders such as Robert Mugabe, Enos Nkala and Leopold Takawira.

I was told that I was entitled to see one visitor a month, and to write one letter a week, which was subject to censorship. There were three categories of meals, i.e. one for whites which was superior, the second category was for coloureds and the most meagre was for blacks – sadza and vegetables or beans. I was advised by prison officials that if I wanted a better diet and bedding, I could get a recommendation from a doctor. I was not prepared to do it. It was a tactic they used to divide us. I told them that this is the kind of discrimination we are fighting against and it will strengthen our resolve to fight until final victory.

As it was at Gonakudzingwa, almost all ethnic groups were represented, mostly from the rural areas in Matabeleland and Mashonaland. In the early years of the struggle rural people were more politically active, because the ANC emphasized the land issue. Nkomo had great support in the rural areas. My background as a former headmaster, president and secretary-general of RATA made me conspicuous. We accepted that we were hostages and that we should be prepared to remain where we were for a very long time. The prison lay between two railway lines, one connecting Harare and Bulawayo and the other leading to Masvingo. There was a main road leading to the so-called African townships. In the first few months the noise from the railways and the road traffic was a serious nuisance but we got used to it.

1959. Banda was detained in Gwelo Prison.

Wherever and whenever human beings congregate, some order has to be created. Gwelo Prison was no exception. Those who held positions of responsibility before they were arrested assumed roughly the same positions inside the prison. I was given the role of organising school classes. Some of the detainees were completely illiterate. I wrote letters to their families and read them the replies. I used the exchange of letters to encourage them to learn to read and write. Within a year almost everyone was literate. We managed to get the International Defence and Aid Fund in the United Kingdom to supply us with learning materials and enrolment fees for those who were studying by correspondence. Phyllis Altman, our contact there, was wonderful. She worked tirelessly to provide everything we needed for our studies.

Our cells were opened at 9 a.m. to allow us to spend time in a courtyard. We were locked up again at 4 p.m. So for seven hours we were left to do whatever we wanted, apart, of course, from trying to escape. There were always two guards watching our movements. Some of them became our friends and were very helpful in smuggling letters we did not want to have censored. We wrote letters to Amnesty International, which took a great interest in our welfare. Inside Rhodesia, Christian Care and its head, the Rev. Steven Manguni, looked after our families. They mobilised funds to assist with school fees, rentals, food, and clothing. Manguni became a household name, working under constant intimidation and harassment, but bringing comfort to our families. We in detention and restriction centres felt extremely indebted to these people who reacted whenever a distress call was made.

We organised classes very seriously. The students regarded detention as a rare and wonderful opportunity to learn. I embarked in 1966 on a Bachelor of Administration course with the University of South Africa, majoring in public administration and political science, which I completed in 1970. I also did a course with the

Institute of Public Relations in London. Almost everyone attended classes; we kept ourselves busy and time flew. Life in detention was frustrating and created tensions among the inmates, but by keeping busy, frustration and tension were kept to a minimum. Detainees' wives were pleasantly surprised to discover that their previously illiterate husbands were now able to read and write. We also gave ourselves time to play some indoor games like table tennis, tsoro, draughts and occasionally soccer in the courtyard. One important benefit was that we learnt to live together regardless of differences in ethnicity. I was reminded of the saying by Richard Lovelace, that "stone walls do not a prison make, nor iron bars a cage; minds innocent and quiet take that for an hermitage."

Gwelo Prison was a hermitage for us.

Our education programme had the full recognition of the prison officials, who went to the extent of appointing me as an invigilator during exam time. I made sure that the examinations were conducted properly and efficiently. When the results came, some passed and others failed, as they would do if they were at their homes. I shall always remain proud of our achievements. We included debates and discussions on political issues such as the one-party state and government powers in a free Zimbabwe. The debates were quite heated, particularly on the one-party state issue. The prisoners were deeply divided. But what was important was that people were able to speak freely.

From time to time we had visits from prison pastors and representatives of the International Committee of the Red Cross. As prisoners of conscience, we found this most consoling. The visitors comforted us and told us that the world had not forgotten us and was interested in our welfare.

We also had tragic moments. The worst of these was when one of us, Robert Bhebhe, was taken to Umtali Magistrates' Court to answer charges of recruiting freedom fighters. He was in his early thirties and it never occurred to us that we would never see him again. After a week, we learnt with dismay and shock that he had been found guilty and was hanged. He was not given the right to a lawyer of his own choice, or the opportunity to appeal. His relatives were not allowed to give him a decent burial. This happened to many young people at that time. All that the authorities relied on was the evidence of an informer, whose credibility was questionable. These were ordinary courts, but operating under the state of emergency. After independence, I met Bhebe's wife and daughter. They were a sorry sight. They were not getting support from anyone, and the woman looked like a destitute. I directed her to a government welfare office. Unfortunately she did not come back to me to report progress, or lack of it. My strong suspicion was that she got frustrated and gave up.

Marriages were broken due to the incarceration, although the majority of wives kept their vows. They waited for many years and looked after their families. I know this from personal experience. My wife had three children and my brother to feed, clothe and to educate, and managed it very successfully. She sent one of them, Cephas Junior, to the United States to do his degree studies. He came back home with a BSc and an MSc in Agricultural Engineering. I am very proud of my wife. The Rhodesian authorities had hoped to demoralise us through the break-up of families. They were disappointed that this did not happen. They underestimated our culture of family strength and unity. My wife owed it to my family and hers to remain faithful. Above all, she was convinced that sooner or later we would be free.

5

Freed from Prison

One day in December 1970, I was called to the Superintendent's office in Gwelo Prison and told that I was being released immediately. Members of the Special Branch were present and reminded me that my movements would be under close
watch. They warned that any disturbances of a political nature
would be attributed to former detainees like me, and we would
have to prove that we were not involved. They did not bother to
arrange transport for me back to Salisbury. I received the news
with mixed feelings. I was filled with joy to know that I was free
to join my family, but sad to leave my friends behind, the majority
of whom had been imprisoned before me. I knew that they would
miss my companionship as much as I would miss theirs. They had
also lost their head teacher!

From the gates of the prison I went straight to my brother
Thomas, a teacher in Ascot township in Gwelo and therefore my
most regular visitor, and he provided me with the bus fare to Salisbury. Charlotte wasn't sure if she was dreaming when she saw

me a few hours later at the front door of our home in Mufakose. It was wonderful and exciting to be together again after five very long years. My youngest son, Charles, was not amused though, as it meant his mother would no longer be able to devote all her attention to him. When I was arrested in 1965, he was a seven-month-old infant. Now he was five and he wished I would go back to prison. He kept on asking Charlotte, "When is this man going back?"

People viewed me differently now. For blacks I was a hero because I had suffered for my country and stood up to the oppressors. To whites, I was dangerous and viewed with suspicion. The blacks had nothing for me except sympathy, love and friendship. Most whites called us terrorists, and saw us as a threat to their comfortable lives.

What I wanted immediately was a job. Teaching was out of the question; the Rhodesian government had sacked me publicly, and would be committing a kind of surrender by taking me on in the service again.

So I got a job at Lobels, the biggest bakery in the country, as an accounts clerk. I found it completely boring. I had undergone training in accounts in prison, but I didn't master much of it because I hated what I was doing. Bennie Lobel, the owner of the business, would pass by my desk and proudly tell visiting South African friends, "This boy of mine is a graduate!" Although he said this with pride, his use of the hateful term "boy" left me feeling very bitter. But my family had to eat and I had to play my role as a breadwinner. So I said nothing.

It was also in 1971 when Aleke Banda, a minister in the Malawi government of Dr Hastings Kamuzu Banda, visited my family. We knew him from Que Que, where he was educated up to Standard 6. We talked about the role Dr Banda could play in our fight against the Rhodesian government of Prime Minister Ian Smith, who had told the whole world that there would be no majority rule in Rhodesia "in a thousand years", though he later shortened this to "not in my lifetime." Aleke was very close to Dr Banda and was extremely intelligent. He had been an active member, at a very tender age, of the Malawi Congress Party. Before he left us, he asked if I would like to meet Dr Banda. I said jubilantly, "Yes, I would love to meet the Ngwazi!"

A week later I received what sounded like an order to come to Malawi. Two air tickets were issued for me and a colleague of my choice to meet Dr Banda in Blantyre. The date and time were fixed. I invited my friend George Kahari.

Soon after we arrived, we were taken to Sanjika Palace, President Banda's residence, where we had serious deliberations with the Ngwazi for ninety minutes. He was on talking terms with Ian Smith as well as John Vorster, the South African prime minister, so we asked him if he could persuade them to open discussions with Joshua Nkomo and Robert Mugabe. His response was that he was in favour of majority rule in Zimbabwe but preferred diplomacy to confrontation. But he agreed to approach Vorster and Smith.

We told him we knew of his reputation as "the destroyer of the Federation [of Rhodesia and Nyasaland]". It was his most repeated claim to fame, and it made him very happy to hear it from us. It was my first meeting with an African head of state, and it opened my eyes. We received VIP treatment throughout our stay and were given a trip to Lake Malawi. I shall never forget that trip. We had to go to Malawi in order to be treated like human beings.

Two months later I got another invitation, to attend the Malawian Congress Party Conference. I was allowed to bring two others, so I invited George Kahari again, but as a member of ZAPU, and Nelson Mawema, a senior member of Ndabaningi Sithole's ZANU, in an attempt to foster unity between the two parties. At the banquet we were asked to stand, so that all the guests could see us. The gesture also served to demonstrate that Banda was not isolated, but had friends outside Malawi. There was a state banquet where the Ngwazi took the opportunity to remind his guests of his reputation as "the destroyer of the Federation".

Again we enjoyed every minute of our stay and wished we could have remained longer. We tasted Malawi's hospitality and enjoyed chambo, the delicious fish that inhabits Lake Malawi. We flew back and deep in our hearts we were singing "memories are made of this".

When I got to the office the following day a khaki envelope was waiting for me and the white manager came to tell me that my services with Lobels had been terminated. "Your involvement in politics will spoil the cordial race relations in our company", he said. It was embarrassing and humiliating. I was treated like a criminal, a trespasser. I was escorted off the premises by a security guard while the manager watched. I went straight home and lay down on my bed. I dreaded telling Charlotte what had happened, but she took it calmly as I told her that I was fired because of our visit to Blantyre. We talked about the constant humiliation we underwent. "This is why we must fight on", I said to myself. Insults like this were an encouragement.

A few days later Victor Cohen – a Jewish friend who published a newsletter for teachers – arranged a meeting between me and Mr John Hillis, a director at David Whitehead, one of the country's major textile companies in Hartley and Gatooma. He was British and a gentleman. He was also partially disabled. He couldn't understand how the the government could keep a person in prison for five years and do nothing to ease his return into normal society. He promised that he would speak with his colleagues about giving me a job.

They agreed to employ me, but they could not agree on what I should do because they did not know where to place me among the whites who dominated the company. David Whitehead was a British company whose main shareholder was the wealthy Tiny Rowland, who made no secret of his support for majority rule in Africa. He was a great friend of Joshua Nkomo and many African leaders, and backed the liberation struggle financially and morally. Eventually I was employed as a public relations manager. Positions like this, and assistant sales manager, were jobs given to blacks because there wasn't much room for them to clash with whites. I worked with African peasant farmers in what were called Tribal Trust Lands,[1] encouraging them to grow cotton, and with women's clubs, persuading them to use David Whitehead's colourful cotton fabrics. I really enjoyed my time with the company, spending a great deal of it in the rural areas. I organised fashion shows. It was great fun, but I also watched change taking place. In Gokwe it was dramatic. The liberation struggle was being intensified. Some areas became dangerous. At Mukumbura in Mashonaland Central among the people at a fashion show there were freedom fighters who warned me never to organise such shows in what they called "liberated zones" again. As a matter of fact I visited every part of Zimbabwe except Binga and Kariba's rural districts which were inaccessible, and had no roads and no business centres. Elsewhere, lifestyles were changing. School uniforms were now made of local fabrics rather than imported fabrics, for instance. In this way we promoted the cash economy and development in the rural areas. Women enjoyed participating in dressmaking competitions. They designed and sewed dresses for themselves in fabrics from the company, competed and won prizes at fashion shows. I employed women demonstrators to teach classes how to sew dresses using special patterns made by the company.

However, we were still under a national state of emergency. There were skirmishes in 1974 between the guerrillas and the

---

1   Renamed Communal Areas in 1982.

Rhodesian security forces. In some areas like Mukumbura, people were held in what were called "keeps", which were protected villages barricaded, fenced and heavily guarded, to deny the guerillas and the people access to each other. More and more people, especially young people, were crossing the borders to join ZIPRA and ZANLA, the military forces of ZAPU and ZANU, ZIPRA in Zambia and ZANLA in Mozambique.

Sanctions had been in force for nearly ten years, but were not producing the required results, as the Rhodesians appeared to be able to circumvent the restrictions easily, largely by importing through South Africa and Mozambique, which was still under Portuguese rule.

The British government was making frantic efforts to restore normality by talking to Smith, and urging him to swallow his pride and talk to Joshua Nkomo and Robert Mugabe. Towards the end of 1971 Smith held talks with the British Prime Minister Alec Douglas-Home which culminated in proposals for conditions to settle the country's political crisis. They were seen as effectively endorsing the continuation of white rule. The British proposed – and the Rhodesian government agreed to – an independent commission to test African opinion throughout the country to determine whether the proposals would be accepted by the majority of the people.

Prior to the appointment of the commission, Douglas-Home visited Rhodesia and arrangements were made to fly Joshua Nkomo and his team from Gonakudzingwa and Robert Mugabe and his team from Salisbury Prison. He met each group separately. I also led a group of former detainees to meet him. We all rejected the proposals because they fell short of our demands for immediate majority rule. Douglas-Home flew back to London and appointed Lord Pearce, a British judge, to head the commission in November 1971. Smith had told the world that the proposals would get overwhelming support from blacks because, he claimed, "We have the happiest Africans in the world."

A month later the African National Council was formed, specifically to urge Africans to reject the Anglo-Rhodesian Proposals. The ANC's founding members were Josiah Chinamano, Amon Jirira and myself from PF ZAPU, and Michael Mawema, Eddison Sithole and Eddison Zvobgo from ZANU.

We agreed to use the heads of churches and trade unions, backed by PF ZAPU and ZANU structures, to mobilise people.

We decided to ask Bishop Abel Muzorewa to lead the new movement, with the Rev. Canaan Banana as his deputy. None of us knew much about Muzorewa except that he was a bishop of the American-based United Methodist Church in the country and had spoken out strongly against white oppression. I was tasked to invite him to head the campaign to reject the Anglo-Rhodesian proposals.

I went to meet him at his luxurious official home in the wealthy black suburb of Marimba Park and found he was not keen to enter politics, and he feared that his church members would find themselves divided along political lines. I explained that the African National Council was not a political party. It was an organisation with the specific function of mobilising opposition to the constitutional proposals. After a long discussion he asked me to give him one week during which he would pray for God's guidance. I left and was confident that he would accept the appointment. After one week I went to see him again and he told me that he was ready to go into battle. Little did we know that in six short years he would be sharing the government of Rhodesia with Ian Smith.

***

Early in 1972 the Pearce Commission criss-crossed the country in the full glare of the media in an effort to gauge African opinion regarding the proposals. Everywhere the result was the same.

It was a huge NO, "Kwete" in Shona and "Asifuni" in Ndebele, as thousands of people came to the gathering places to register their opinions peacefully, and jubilantly. It was spectacular to see multitudes of people waiting to express their opposition to the proposals. In May that year, Pearce reported that African opinion was overwhelmingly opposed to the proposed Rhodesian constitution. Douglas-Home commented that there was need for "time for reflection" on the result, and said that the problems of Rhodesia needed to be solved by Rhodesians themselves – and not just the whites.

Smith ignored his advice. In the process thousands of lives were lost unnecessarily between 1972 and December 1980 when final agreement on proposals to end the conflict in Rhodesia was reached by all the parties to the Lancaster House conference in London.

The response to the Pearce Commission was an important political statement because it gave Africans the power to exercise their right to determine the future of their country. International voices against Rhodesia, encouraged by the Organisation of African Unity (OAU) and the Frontline States, were growing increasingly loud in their condemnation of the Rhodesian regime. Smith, however, assured his supporters that nothing would change. Mugabe and Nkomo were back in their respective prisons in Salisbury and Gonakudzingwa, but pressure was mounting for their release.

Simultaneously, the trickle of teenage boys and girls running away from their homes and schools to join the liberation struggle had turned into a flood. The Soviet Union and China increased their support for ZIPRA and ZANLA. Even Smith's closest allies, the South African government, were warning him that he was fighting a losing battle.

Smith eventually agreed to attend an international conference on South Africa's luxury "White Train" parked in the middle of the bridge over the Zambezi River, the boundary between Rhodesia and Zambia. The meeting took place on 25 August 1975. It was monitored by big names from the Frontline States, while Zambia's President Kaunda and South African Prime Minister John Vorster chatted on the sidelines. Mugabe and Nkomo and their senior aides were released from detention to attend.

Later in 1975 Dr Nkomo received information that Smith was prepared to reconsider his position on majority rule. He then agreed to meet Smith and proposed an immediate transition to an interim government leading to majority rule. After a few weeks, the talks broke down as had been the case in Geneva and Victoria Falls. Nkomo was a man of peace and was prepared to pursue whatever route could lead to peace. After this, guerrilla incursions picked up strongly because of Smith's intransigents.

***

I was at home when I heard a familiar voice from the kitchen, instructing my wife to prepare a meal quickly. Mugabe! I had not seen him for ten years. He was barely an hour out of Salisbury prison and had taken a bus ride direct to my home in Mufakose. After he finished eating, he said, "Let's go, Sekuru," and told my wife not to expect me back early. As we got into into my car, I asked him where we were going. Clearly there would be no sight-seeing. He said he had a list of names of people he needed to see that day. As I drove, we talked of his experiences in prison (although he did not tell me he had been elected there to be the leader of ZANU to replace Ndabaningi Sithole) and he asked about the political climate in the country. We stopped at several houses in the neighbouring township of Kambuzuma. He did not tell me who he was seeing and I did not ask. I had no doubt they were ZANU members. Our relationship was personal and we avoided meddling in each other's territory. On several occasions before he had raised the issue of our membership of opposing parties. In

1963 we had agreed to disagree, and I told him I would not be joining ZANU. He didn't ask me about PF ZAPU. When we got to the last house on his list, he thanked me, asked me to leave him there and told me to go straight back home. His dedication and commitment amazed me. Most people would set aside a few days to see relatives. Not Mugabe. The most important thing in his mind was the prosecution of the war.

Soon after this, my boss at David Whitehead Textiles wanted to know how the African nationalists planned to run the country when, and if, they took power. I invited Mugabe and Nkomo to a confidential meeting at our offices in Salisbury. They each agreed to come, probably out of respect for their friendship with me. I did not attend but Hillis briefed me. About Mugabe, he said, "He is very intelligent and articulate but is a Marxist and Leninist. If he were to take over there will be no room for the whites." As for Nkomo he said, "He is friendly and reasonable. He can accommodate us."

Joshua Nkomo leaving the Prime Minister's office after talks with Ian Smith, 1 December 1975 (l to r: John Nkomo, Josiah Chinamano, JN, Daniel Madzimbamuto, Clement Muchachi, Chief Mangwende)

Later that year, Mugabe and I next met at Silveira House, the Catholic mission just east of Harare, where he spoke on ZANU's way forward, and I spoke on PF ZAPU's vision of the future. It was a private meeting convened to give the leaders of ZAPU and ZANU the opportunity to explain to a selected audience the critical issues facing our two parties. He was very tense and uncomfortable with me. I could see that he had something worrying him. A few days later I heard that he had crossed to Mozambique, and I realised why he had behaved oddly.

***

In 1975, after the PF ZAPU Central Committee had resolved that all its members move from Harare to Lusaka, Zambia, in order to concentrate on the prosecution of the armed struggle, Nkomo told me that I was to remain in Harare. He wanted me, as ZAPU's secretary for education, to assist students to go abroad for training, in addition to looking after the party's interests. Thus, I worked from the ANC (ZAPU) offices sending several thousands of young people to Zambia via Botswana for further education. We were aware that we could have gone to the gallows for recruiting "freedom fighters".

The education department was two-pronged. There were young, displaced boys and girls who were housed in refugee camps in Zambia, for whom the party established a school at each of the two camps, 'Victory' for girls and 'JZ' for boys. The children were taught by professional teachers who had also joined the struggle, and most of the education materials were provided by UNICEF and the Lutheran World Federation.

The second element, which was more popular and successful, was a scholarship programme for further education and manpower development for students recruited directly from Rhodesia and deployed via Botswana to Zambia, from where they could apply for scholarships to socialist countries, like the Soviet Union and

Bulgaria.The scholarship progamme was co-ordinated by Thenjiwe Lesabe and Phibion Makoni in Lusaka.

The Zambian government, in collaboration with Commonwealth, each year provided sponsorship for hundreds of students to do commercial courses at Nkumbi International College at Kapiri Mposhi and Kasama College of Education, both in Zambia. Under Commonwealth sponsorship we were also able to send students to Nigeria, Kenya, Jamaica, Trinidad and Tobago, and Tanzania. In co-operation with the Commonwealth, PF ZAPU established a secretarial college at Kafue in southern Zambia where hundreds of girls were trained.

What is important is that as a result of the education they acquired, they were able to make a meaningful contribution to the development of the country. Zimbabwe is a big exporter of skilled manpower I am pleased that I have been able to make a small contribution to the success story of human development. Let us continue to commit ourselves to eradicating ignorance and to look at education as a basic human right.

***

Bishop Muzorewa was now enjoying being president of the ANC, which was the only black political organisation permitted. Some of us took a back seat. He went to the point of appointing John Nkomo and Simon Muzenda – at the time members of the reformed ANC – to open an office in Lusaka. As soon as they got to Lusaka, each immediately reconnected with their respective parties. Before long, Bishop Muzorewa renamed his party the United African National Council, apparently aiming to establish himself as the leader of a third African force against the Rhodesian government. It got short shrift from the Frontline States.

The war gained momentum and the guerrilla incursions were increasing at an alarming rate. The guerillas were welcomed in the rural areas, where the people sheltered and fed them. They nicknamed them "vakomana" (the boys). The military keeps that the Rhodesian authorities had created did not dampen their spirits. The war moved into Salisbury, with the bombing of Woolworths store in August 1977, and the destruction of Rhodesia's main fuel depot in December 1978.

Mr Hillis asked me to arrange an audience with Bishop Muzorewa. The meeting took place at the Bishop's home in Marimba Park. Hillis briefed me the following day. He was full of praise for Muzorewa, and went on to tell me that he would make sure that the Bishop met Smith. I immediately regretted that I had introduced them. Hillis did bring Muzorewa and Smith together, and it was the beginning of an alliance between the two which culminated in the formation in 1978 of the Government of National Unity between Muzorewa's UANC and Smith's Rhodesian Front. The reaction to this political alignment was that we no longer needed to recruit people into the struggle. All they wanted was to know how to get to Mozambique or Zambia to join the military forces.

In October, 1976, British Prime Minister James Callaghan convened another all-party conference, though this one would actually last more than a day, in Geneva and under the chairmanship of Sir Ivor Richard. The nationalist parties ZANU and PF ZAPU were invited under the leadership of Robert Mugabe and Joshua Nkomo respectively, but under the joint banner of the Patriotic Front. Parties from Rhodesia were represented by Ian Smith (Rhodesian Front), Bishop Muzorewa (UANC), Ndabaningi Sithole (ZANU Ndonga)[2] and James Chikerema (FROLIZI).[3] The conference started on 28 October and ended on 14 December, 1976. I attended as part of the Patriotic Front, as a PF ZAPU delegate, for the first time. I was surprised and impressed with the unity of purpose dis-

---

2 A split-off from ZANU formed in 1975, and which renounced violent struggle.
3 The Front for the Liberation of Zimbabwe, a short-lived group formed in 1971 following a split in the leadership of ZAPU.

played at the preliminary meetings between the ZAPU and ZANU sectors of the Patriotic Front. Nkomo and Mugabe co-chaired all the sessions admirably well. I was overjoyed to see the cooperation of our two sides. It seemed that the hostilities and suspicion that had run through our dealings back home had been forgotten in Geneva. Josiah Tongogara, the commander of ZANLA, warned us not to pass on to our children the differences that had grown between us. The much-feared commander left us with the impression that he preferred peace to war.

The first few days of the conference went badly. Even the name "Zimbabwe" was considered provocative by the Rhodesian delegation. At one point the atmosphere became so acrimonious it appeared the the talks would end prematurely. The PF made it clear that majority rule must be accepted or they would continue fighting until the end. Smith was as intransigent as ever. Halfway through the meeting, we were told that the Rhodesians were broadcasting back home that no progress was being made because the PF was making unreasonable demands and was determined on a course of bloodshed rather than peace. Nkomo immediately sent me back to Rhodesia to give our side of the story.

On my way home, however, I made a brief stopover in London where I addressed a meeting of students from Rhodesia. Many of them were rowdy and accused the PF leaders of betraying the armed struggle. They condemned the recent negotiations with Ian Smith in Geneva, and insisted that war was the only way forward. In reply, I told them that many young people of their age were leaving their studies to go to either Mozambique or Zambia to join the forces of liberation. I promised them that I could organise their travel to either of the two countries, if they genuinely wanted to go. I appealed to them to come and offer themselves as fighters. None came forward, and the agitators left the meeting quietly. I was able to address the remaining students without interruption.

As soon as I reached home, PF ZAPU organised meetings, mostly in Harare and Bulawayo, at which we briefed our supporters on what had happened at the Geneva conference. I led the team in Harare, and Vote Moyo, a ZAPU central committee member, led the discussions in Bulawayo. Our main objective was to neutralise the Rhodesians' propaganda. Finally, after six frustrating weeks, the Geneva Conference was adjourned indefinitely. We had not expected any other outcome.

The conference had one important result. The unity in the Patriotic Front's organisation was strengthened. We met regularly in Geneva under the joint chairmanship of Nkomo and Mugabe and discussed our strategies together. We got to know each other more and built some trust. We made friends and mingled socially. It was like a rehearsal for the final push at the Lancaster House conference that was to come in 1979. The time spent together in Geneva temporarily strengthened the relationship between ZAPU and ZANU.

6

From Geneva to Lancaster House

B ut in other ways the Geneva Conference was a waste of time. It
appears that delegates were not sure what to expect of the conference. Sir Ivor Richard was not able to bring about any cohesion.
It took weeks for the conference to start. We haggled over minor
issues for days on end. Even after it got underway, progress was
at a snail's pace. It was like strangers meeting. We were a group
of disparate organisations, each made up of people who did not
relate to each other in any way, did not understand each other's
point of view, and weren't interested anyway.

Smith decided to re-strategise. He had got to know Muzorewa
and Chikerema better in Geneva, and decided to work with them.
In June 1979 they formed a government of national unity, with
ministers drawn from the various parties, and Bishop Muzorewa
as prime minister. They couldn't even agree on a name, so they
settled on Zimbabwe-Rhodesia (although many of the whites insisted on Rhodesia-Zimbabwe).

Back in Salisbury, John Hillis, my boss at David Whitehead,

called me in to his office and asked me, "Are you still supporting those terrorists?", meaning Nkomo and, especially, Mugabe. When I answered "yes", he said, "In that case, if you support terrorists, it will make our work difficult for the company. We are happy with the present arrangement between Muzorewa and Smith and we are going to work with that government." I explained to Hillis why I supported Mugabe and Nkomo. I said as long they hadn't come to the peace table, as long as there is no majority rule, there wouldn't be peace in Zimbabwe, and it didn't make sense to prolong the suffering of the people. For that reason, I said, I would continue to support them.

He advised me to look for another job. Fortunately, I had recently found that my friend, Herbert Munangatire, had started a newspaper, the *Zimbabwe Times* which was funded by Tiny Rowland. Munangatire was too busy to edit it, so he asked me to run the paper. We had worked together at African Newspapers and he was confident of my experience. I penned a column, "I Write As I Please", which proved to be very popular.

The hopes of Mr Hillis, and of Murozewa, Smith and the rest of the Zimbabwe-Rhodesia government, were not to last. In August 1979, just less than a year after the formation of Zimbabwe-Rhodesia, Margaret Thatcher was at the Commonwealth Conference in Lusaka and won consensus from the organisation for another all-party conference to try, for once and for all, to resolve the Rhodesian conflict.

Both the American and South African governments were lending their weight to finding a resolutiont. Even Chief Jeremiah Chirau, the head of the Council of Chiefs and for years regarded as a Rhodesian Front stooge, spoke out in support of the conference. I published a statement from him in the *Zimbabwe Times*. "The question of inheritance according to African tradition and culture was very important and could not be settled in the absence of other children," he said. "Therefore, if a settlement is to be found on the Rhodesian issue, Cde Mugabe and Cde Nkomo have to be there. Anything less would be unacceptable." For a change, Chirau found himself enthusiastically applauded.

Smith and Muzorewa were saying they had formed a government and there was no need to bring in another; instead, it was up to the British to recognise the Zimbabwe-Rhodesia government. However, the international community insisted on the need for an all-party conference.

Josiah Chinamano, the vice-president of PF ZAPU, asked me to see if I could persuade Bishop Muzorewa to accept an invitation to an all-party conference under the chairmanship of the British government. Muzorewa's and Smith's insistence that there already was an elected African-majority government in place, had been ignored internationally, except by South Africa. They were, therefore, almost completely isolated.

I went to see the Bishop at his home, thinking it was going to be a short meeting. It started started at 7 p.m. and went on until 10 p.m. His argument was, "You people persuaded me to come into politics and I did. Now you are saying I should get out?" My reply was, "No, we are not saying 'get out'. All we are saying is, let's go and agree on a constitution, then we can participate in a general election and whoever wins can run the country. You and Smith have no mandate to run the country." He complained that we were making him look like a schoolboy being given orders by his teachers.

As we went on he made what I thought was a terrible tactical blunder. He said, "Are you aware that there are people in this country who are prepared to die for me?" I was stunned. I asked him angrily to repeat it, and he did. I told him that was a shocking statement for a Bishop to make. I said that Mugabe and Nkomo had thousands of young men and women who were prepared to die for their freedom – and not for Mugabe or Nkomo personally. I said to him, "Do you want all these young people to come before you and agree to attend an all-party conference?" Muzorewa's UANC party had a small militia of irregulars called "Pfumo Revanhu" (Spear of the People). I said that the Patriotic Front forces could wipe out the movement in a day. "But we are for democracy," I said. "We don't want to destroy your tiny army."

It shook him. I had also lost my temper. More calmly now, I said, "Now you know, for a Bishop to boast of people who are willing to die for him, that is really unbelievable and it's ungodly." He then said, "Ah... maybe I didn't put it correctly. Let me withdraw that statement." Then he fell to his knees and prayed. When he had finished, I said, "Right. When then do we meet to know your position on an all-party conference?" He said he was "very busy" that week, preparing for a major speech in South Africa on the significance of Zimbabwe-Rhodesia and he did not want to be disturbed. He asked for a week to think about it, just as he had when we first asked him four years earlier to lead the African National Council against the Smith-Douglas-Home constitutional proposals. He had said then he wanted to pray to God for guidance. This time, however, I knew he wanted advice from Smith and from the South African government.

The government of the "internal settlement" was under unprecedented military pressure. The war was brought home vividly to whites, literally in their own backyard, when guerrillas fired a rocket at one of the tanks at Salisbury's big fuel depot and set the whole storage facility ablaze for days on end. Military conscription had most of the white male population – including men in their 60s – on regular army duty. Then, in an enormously unpopular move, they conscripted young blacks into Rhodesian military uniform. Many – blacks and whites alike – fled the country. Others had no choice but to be conscripted.

The Rhodesian army launched surprise raids on ZANLA bases in Mozambique and on ZIPRA bases in Zambia, killing hundreds.

This was followed by the downing of an Air Rhodesia Viscount passenger plane – the second in a year – by ZIPRA guerrillas using a surface-to-air missile. ZIPRA said afterwards they had believed that General Peter Walls, the commander of the Rhodesian army, was on board. The incident set off a wave of new arrests. I urged my friends Willie Musarurwa and Josiah Chinamano to leave the country immediately as their arrest was imminent. My wife said to me, "You are talking of these people being arrested. What about you?"

"I have spent the day in my office, why would they associate me with the shooting down of the aircraft?"

"Wait and see," she said.

That night there was a loud knock at the door. "Didn't I tell you?" said Charlotte. We opened the door to a group of white officers, five of whom were in plainclothes. They came inside, while several others, in uniform and armed, waited outside.

The five plainclothes men came in and ransacked the house. They turned it upside down, the wardrobes, cupboards, kitchen drawers, beds – everything. When they had finished, they said to my wife, "Yes, we're through now, and we're taking your husband away." My wife was furious. "You are not leaving until you put everything back in the manner you found it." To my astonishment, they did exactly that. When everything was properly restored, they asked her if they could now take me away. She assented.

It was midnight, and I was driven to Lake McIlwaine. I don't know why they took me there. The car stopped and two of them sat with me while the other two went outside for a whispered discussion. I felt sure they were planning to kill me and dump my body in the lake. It was a terrifying moment. But eventually we drove off.

We ended up at a building I did not recognise and I was put in a dark cell. There was a figure there and asked who he was. He recognized my voice straightaway. "Oh, young man, they have picked you too?" It was Eric Gwanzura, a member of ZANU and a former trade unionist. I said, "Yes, and you? When were you picked up?" He said it had been a few hours since, and he also had no clue where we were. No one would tell us where we were. We were kept there for about three days and then taken to Chikurubi Maximum Security Prison east of Salisbury. There were hundreds of us there. Our relatives had no idea where we were. I heard later there were rumours that we had been killed.

Then we were taken to Wha Wha Prison near Gwelo. We were split into two camps, one for ZANU(PF), the other for PF ZAPU. The numbers were swelling every day. I found many friends from both parties there. The two parties talked to each other across the fence, it was very convivial. It was as if the political differences that separated us had suddenly been removed by the prison walls.

***

Each annual Commonwealth Heads of Government Meeting includes a weekend retreat away from microphones and the media, where the leaders can relax and chew the fat in private. It is a perfect opportunity for informal approaches and meetings to happen, and for prickly old problems to be settled over a couple of Scotches, or whatever, without anyone having to look over their shoulder.

The retreat for the Lusaka CHOGM in August 1979 took place in Livingstone, barely a few hundred metres from Rhodesian gun emplacements on the other side of the Zambezi River looking over Victoria Falls. There, Thatcher persuaded the African Commonwealth group, but principally Kaunda and Nyerere, of the need for another attempt at a Rhodesian peace conference, and to put pressure on Nkomo and Mugabe to attend. It was organised in a surprisingly short time.

It was to take place at Lancaster House, a mansion originally built for the Duke of York in the St James's district of London. I got a message to say that Nkomo wanted me to join his delegation. Prison officials at Wha Wha told me I was free to leave. I was happy to leave the prison and swiftly made my way to London.

When I got to Lancaster House, there were emissaries from many countries and organisations, including the vital diplomatic players from the United States and the Frontline States. There was a sense of urgency that hadn't been there at Geneva. Everybody was expecting something to happen. The main focus was on the Patriotic Front led by Joshua Nkomo and Robert Mugabe. They were confident that the armed struggle was having an effect and the international community was behind them, and anxious to end the war and restore peace. They were also well prepared this time, having got to understand each other's positions since their first encounter at Geneva.

Smith and his group from Zimbabwe-Rhodesia were perhaps not as well organised, although they had much more experience at formal meetings like this.

It began amid high expectations on 10 September with Lord Carrington, the British foreign secretary, as chairman. He was confident and capable, and impressed us as a man with a mission to agree on terms of an independent constitution to enable Rhodesia to proceed to lawful and internationally recognised elections. Edison Zvobgo of ZANU(PF) and PF ZAPU's Willie Musarurwa were the spokesmen of the Patriotic Front. They executed their duties extremely well, occupying the airwaves in London as if we were in Salisbury, and kept everybody informed of what was happening. The PF met after each plenary session, sometimes more than once, to review what had transpired and to strategise for the next session. It was exhausting. The conference had been going on for eight weeks when Nkomo called me and said, "It's clear an agreement will be reached. When, I don't know, but there is no way we can fail to come to some agreement. It's also clear that we'll have to go home and have elections. Whether these elections will be under the Patriotic Front or we will stand separately as ZANU(PF) and PF ZAPU we don't know." We did not yet know how crucial this issue was to become.

He asked me to return home and prepare for elections. I left when the conference was into its tenth week, and back home I was immediately accepted by the media as the spokesman of the Patriotic Front. They were anxious to hear first-hand information from someone fresh from Lancaster House.

Shortly before I left London, I was approached by officers of the Rhodesian Special Branch, about five of them. They said there was no chance that the Patriotic Front would stand as a united organisation in the coming elections and that ZANU(PF) would break away to stand on its own, leaving PF ZAPU to contest the elections alone. They predicted that ZANU was certain to win overwhelmingly, except in Matabeleland, while in the Midlands the vote would be more or less evenly split between the two. They made a proposal that PF ZAPU should walk out of the conference as a protest against the way things were going. They didn't want the conference to succeed; they wanted to see a split in the PF. They followed that up with the suggestion that Nkomo and ZIPRA should join forces with Smith and Muzorewa in a military alliance against Mugabe's ZANLA forces.

I told them that it was the most stupid thing anyone could think of. It showed deep misunderstanding between whites and blacks. I dismissed the whole thing and said I would never even discuss it with Dr. Nkomo. He would think I was mad, because there was no way we could stand in front of Africa and be seen to have joined forces with Ian Smith to fight ZANLA. I also reminded them that as far as we were concerned, ZANLA and ZIPRA were one. Some of the members across the political divide were even very close relatives. It was not just a question of bringing an end to minority rule and delivering majority rule, but also of saving the lives of the people. What they were proposing was a whole new phase of a war that had already gone on for 15 years. We did not want one more person to die. We had lost our relatives on both sides and it had to be brought to an end.

In essence, I told them they were talking nonsense and that I would never consider such a thing. I said if their calculations were right that ZANU(PF) would win as opposed to PF ZAPU, that would be the way it ought to be, because that was what democracy was all about. If we did fight separately and ZANU(PF) won, we would welcome the outcome because the election would have been held under the conditions of one-man, one-vote, which was what we had been fighting for.

Back in Salisbury, we kept on promising people that the conference would come to an end soon, but it continued, day after day. I was running short of words. I couldn't go on repeating myself without anything materialising. I went directly to see Chief Chirau, in his capacity as the president of the Chiefs' Council and leader of his party. I wanted him to throw his weight behind PF ZAPU whom I was representing, although the media projected me as the spokesperson of the Patriotic Front. Chirau was happy to provide us with the endorsement we wanted.

Then I went to see Chief Kayisa Ndiweni, a leading paramount chief in Matabeleland. He came straight out: "What is your policy, is it unitary government or a federal one?" I told him we wanted a unitary system.

"In that case you can count me out," he said. "There is no way I can support that kind of government for Zimbabwe." I asked why.

"Because it will mean that Joshua Nkomo can never be president of Zimbabwe. By virtue of numbers, we Ndebele will always be a minority. Therefore if we support a federal type of government the chances are that he will be a leader."

I argued with him, but it was clear he had been thinking about the issue for some time and was not prepared to budge.

I told Nkomo. "You cannot persuade Chief Ndiweni to support a unitary system," he said. "I've heard his views before. I didn't think we would get much co-operation from him. Let's go ahead."

I had to organise meetings of PF ZAPU, but the police still weren't allowing party rallies. So we would pretend we were holding press conferences although there would be hundreds of people present. The police would turn up and ask me where the journalists were. I would point to the crowds around us. I was charged with holding illegal meetings on several occasions, but the charges were withdrawn after the general elections in February.

Ian Smith had also returned home before the conclusion of the talks. I had never met him preivately, so I was taken aback when I got a telephone call from his secretary. "Mr. Smith would like to meet you."

I was intrigued, so I went to his office in Milton Buildings. He did not shake my hand. He maintained his composure, but sounded like a man who had accepted defeat.

He asked, "Are you in touch with Nkomo and Mugabe?" I said I spoke with Nkomo every day.

"What are they still doing in London?"

"Still talking," I replied. "The land issue hasn't been solved. There are still problems there."

"So they want the British to make laws for us? Do they not know that the Patriotic Front is going to run this country?"

It's possible, but we want to make sure that everything is in place."

"Look," he said, "I have surrendered, that is why I am here. Muzorewa is finished. I don't know what he is doing in London.

What remains is for you people to come and hold elections and run the country."

He asked me to tell Nkomo not to waste his time on the land issue. It could be resolved by the parties back home. "Who else is going to stand in your way as the PF?"

What he was saying made sense to me. He was clear in his mind that the PF was going to form the next government and that it would have the power to make or amend any law, including on land ownership. So why involve the British in something that the PF could do after the elections?

Afterwards I had a long discussion with Nkomo. He was suspicious. "I don't believe him. Why do you trust him?"

"It's not that I trust him, but when he acknowledges that we are going to take over the running of this country, why should I not trust him?" I insisted that it was important to consider what Smith was saying. But Nkomo rejected his suggestions out of hand.

Interestingly, when Smith and I had finished our discussion, he asked me to take care, when I spoke to Nkomo about our meeting, to speak in Shona or Ndebele, but not in English. "I don't want the British to know that I am advising you people. They hate me. If they think I am advising you, they will then tell you to take a different route altogether." I agreed.

The PF was not about to accept any advice from Smith, as Nkomo had dismissed it. But on the other hand I thought what he was saying made sense. In fact, what he was saying was what actually happened.

Salisbury was tense at this time, and being the public representative of the PF made me a marked man. In early December 1979 a man with an American accent called me on my home phone number at Lochinvar, swore at me and told me I was about to die. He phoned again later in the day and said several people had come from America to kill me.

Three days later I was sitting in bed when a shot rang out, and a bullet lodged in the wall just next to my head. Then the sound of a car speeding away. I called the police. They came the next day and while they were there, the phone rang and a strange voice asked me, "Do you remember the Viscount?"

"What do I have to do with the Viscount?" I countered. He hung up.

Then a couple of days later, someone called saying he was answering an advertisement in the *Rhodesia Herald*, offering a rifle for sale. I thought they must have called a wrong number, but after 20 or so more calls, I realised it wasn't. Later I found the advedrtisement in the paper. It was offering an M16 assault rifle with two rounds of ammunition, and specifying: "will be used twice." It gave my phone number.

Death threats disturb Msipa

$\text{\small Herald Reporter}$ man with an American

The Herald, 5 December, 1979

The Lancaster House talks dragged on and on, but at last, on 21 December, after 16 weeks, agreement was reached and all the parties signed. For me back in Zimbabwe-Rhodesia (as it still was) the immediate effect was that the police no longer had any right to charge me for calling "illegal meetings".

I had to concentrate on organising for Nkomo's return home in early 1980. It created a lot of problems for me. He had told me to organise accommodation in Salisbury, where he would be based. I contacted several friends who were delighted to offer him a temporary home, free of charge. But as the day drew nearer for his arrival, one by one they came to say, sorry, they could not accommodate him. I asked them why. "He's a security risk," they said.

"Surely they were aware of this when you made the offer?" "Aahh, we are being told our whole family would be wiped out. We can't have him."

I tried hotels. The message was the same. "Keep your money, we don't want it. We can't have Nkomo, our property would be destroyed."

I reported back to Nkomo telling him that no one wanted to have him.

"Don't you have a house yourself?"

"Yes," I said. "I have a small house, in an area where railway workers used to live, so it's very small."

"I'm coming to join you in that small house," he said.

I prepared a bedroom for him. I bought a bed which would befit his status, a double bed with springs to make sleeping comfortable. I showed him the bedroom. He looked around and said, "What about my secretaries?"

I said they could have the room next to his bedroom. Then he said, "Yes, but what about S.K. Moyo [his special personal assistant] and Nxele [head of his security aides]? They must be next to me."

This was too much. "Old man," I said. "You are now creating problems. This house has three bedrooms; if I give you those three bedrooms it means my wife and I will have nowhere to sleep."

"It's your problem," he said.

I called Charlotte. She said we should give up the three bedrooms. "And where are we and the children going to sleep?" I demanded.

"Leave it to me," she said. "I will talk to our neighbours. Somehow they will accommodate us."

The neighbours agreed to accommodate our children. Charlotte and I moved into our domestic quarters for the period that

Nkomo was our guest.

***

We were out of the house but still we had to look after Nkomo and his entourage. We had to do with what little we had. I had lost my job with David Whitehead, the *Zimbabwe Times* had been banned, I had no income. My wife had her teacher's salary and friends helped from time to time, particularly while Nkomo was our guest. Every day Charlotte would make sure Nkomo and his entourage had breakfast, lunch and supper. Lunch was the most problematic because people who came to see him expected to be fed as well. But Charlotte was very understanding. So was Nkomo. It was a major undertaking for us, but we were proud of doing it.

The little house in Lochinvar

And before long my little house in Lochinvar, 5 Palm Crescent, had become a refugee camp with hundreds of people. With the country irrevocably heading for independence, and the end of racist white minority rule, people were pouring back home through the country's northern, eastern and western borders. Young people who had been in PF ZAPU camps in Zambia were among them, and their first port of call was my house. I arranged transport for them to their homes by bus, train, taxi, whatever, but I tell you, it was really busy. The toilets blocked. Nothing was working.

At the same time, we were looking for a house for Nkomo. He specifically wanted a house in Highfield township, not in the white suburbs. He wanted to be among the people. After a few days we got one, in Old Highfeild, a big house built on a large stand.

The Lancaster House Agreement was now in operation. Zimbabwe-Rhodesia, the international polecat, was no more and the country was directly ruled by Britain, under the governor, Lord Soames. The elaborate plans, agreed at Lancaster House, for pre-independence arrangements were unfolding, including a ceasefire, the release of political prisoners and preparations for an election under the system of proportional representation. There was clearly no time to carry out voter registration.

So Ian Smith's UDI came to an end. In 1965, the British had predicted it would be just a matter of weeks before it collapsed but the illegal regime lasted 15 years and created a major international crisis which involved almost the whole world, with the East, the West and, of course, Africa striving for a resolution. The cost was too ghastly to contemplate. The loss of lives and destruction to the Frontline States was incalculable.

The Frontline leaders were very relieved that the whole long episode was over, so they could now concentrate on ending apartheid in South Africa, and looking forward to a free Africa, from Cape to Cairo

The fighters from the guerrilla armies were ordered by their commanders to move into official assembly points, scattered in remote areas around the country, to ensure they would not influence the running of the election and the political parties' campaigns. The Rhodesian army troops were confined to their barracks.

Five days after the signing of the agreement in London, on Boxing Day, 41 ZANLA commanders arrived in Salisbury from Maputo under the leadership of Rex Nhongo, their deputy commander. A similar number of ZIPRA commanders arrived shortly after that from Zambia under the leadership of Dumiso Dabengwa, the movement's head of military intelligence, and Lookout Masuku, the overall commander. Many thousands of delirious supporters, coming from every direction, most of them on foot and in a joyful, peaceful mood, jammed Salisbury Airport, oblivious to police roadblocks and police dogs. A Rhodesian army unit had mounted machine-gun nests around the airport and I had to get them moved out of sight. The people wanted to welcome their liberators.

The British had asked both PF ZAPU and ZANU(PF) to be part of the welcoming party. But as the planes landed, ZANU(PF)'s officials were nowhere to be seen. It turned out that the locally-based leadership were squabbling over whether Enos Nkala or James Bassopo-Moyo should head the welcoming party. Nkala claimed that he had suspended Basoppo-Moyo for "challenging his leadership".

In their absence, it was left to me to receive the ZANLA commanders and to escort them to the University of Rhodesia where they were temporarily accommodated. They appeared confused and subdued and did not share the excitement of the huge crowd that welcomed them at the airport. I did not tell them why no ZANU(PF) leaders had turned up.

I had not thought to wonder why Josiah Tongogara, ZANLA's commander, was not on the flight. He was supposed to have arrived together with Dabengwa on a British chartered plane. Dabengwa said nothing to me. Only the next day did I discover that Tongogara had been killed in a road accident in Mozambique. He had been on his way to Maputo to catch the flight to Salisbury as the head of the ZANLA group. This explained why the other ZANLA officers were troubled. But they had also said nothing.

PF ZAPU was as shocked as ZANU(PF) about Tongogara's

death. We considered him to be a moderate in his party, and much more pragmatic than many of his colleagues. His views carried a great deal of weight.

My own interaction with him in Geneva and at Lancaster House left me with the impression of a leader prepared for unity under the Patriotic Front. He was always very warm towards me, and affectionately called me "mudhara" (old man).

Nkomo was profoundly shocked by the death of Josiah Tongogara. It was thought that Nkomo's chances as co-leader of the Patriotic Front in the coming elections would have been better had Tongogara been alive. His death robbed us all of a great leader with a vision of a united people.

The following day, I received congratulatory messages from foreign diplomats in my capacity as spokesperson of the Patriotic Front. The first, surprisingly, was from the diplomatic representative in Salisbury of South Africa's apartheid-ruled government. All the diplomats were saying that the thousands of supporters at the airport left them in no doubt that the Patriotic Front was going to win the election by a big majority. I felt great.

But by this time we had learnt, from an announcement by Enos Nkala, that ZANU was going to fight the elections on its own, and not as part of the Patriotic Front. We were not surprised, though, as the union had been seen as a loose arrangement to fight the war as a joint force, and for the negotiations for a new constitution, even though Mugabe and Nkmo had signed the Lancaster House document as representatives of the Patriotic Front. There had never been any formal, written agreement on the union. It was more of an expression of intent. There were also differences of policy, with ZANU(PF)'s inclination toward socialism – insisting, for example, that party leaders would not be allowed to own more than 15 hectares of land, although this was quickly reversed.

Furthermore, ZANU(PF) was much more inclined to being

ruled by a small group at the top, and did not permit much debate. ZAPU was far more open and tolerant.

Nkomo had told me when he first sent me back from London, to campaign for the PF and work together with ZANU(PF), but added, "Don't put all your eggs in one brasket." We also knew there was no unanimity in ZANU(PF) on the issue.

It was significant, though, that the announcement came from Nkala, who had never gone to Lancaster House but had stayed in Zimbabwe. Mugabe had said nothing about it to Nkomo. Nkomo accepted it.

Nkomo finally came back home on 13 January after three years in exile. I was given the task of organising a homecoming rally for him at Zimbabwe Grounds in Highfield, his first rally in a free Zimbabwe. I found it the most challenging task. I had never had to arrange as anything as big as this, nor did I have the manpower or the finance to carry it out. Between 100,000 and 150,000 supporters turned up, and it was a wonderful occasion, and the atmosphere was joyous.

The turnout for Mugabe, at the same venue, however, was significantly more when he came home a couple of weeks later. I hadn't had the back-up to match ZANU(PF)'s, and most of the ZAPU top brass were still out of the country. But it was an immediate and clear indicator of where the most votes would go.

Elections for 80 of the seats in the proposed 100-member parliament were held all over the country from 27 to 29 February.[1] There were huge queues all over and the mood generally was joyous.

I had been campaigning and supervising voting for PF ZAPU in Midlands Province, where a big fight had been expected between my party and ZANU(PF), as it was probably the only area in the country where the two parties were evenly matched in support.

---

1   Elections for the 20 white seats had been held on February 14.

Nkomo should have been representing PF ZAPU there. ZANU(PF) didn't have a hope in Bulawayo so he should not have bothered to contest there; he should have campaigned in the Midlands. His presence could well have secured it for us. But he didn't, and that's history. ZANU(PF) had deployed Mugabe's deputy, Simon Muzenda as their drawcard.

As I drove back to Harare that night, I asked my wife, "What do you think the outcome will be?" She told me without hesitation that ZANU(PF) was going to win overwhelmingly.

I was not very surprised because I knew their election strategy and that the methods they used were such that they were bound to win. Contrary to rules laid down by Lord Soames, ZANLA fighters were widely deployed in many areas outside their assembly points.

In Midlands Province, for instance, I had heard that ZANLA had camped just across the bridge that links Zvishavane and Mberengwa. When I made an attempt to cross there into into Mberengwa, ZANU(PF) cadres carrying AK-47 rifles threatened me and ordered me to go back and never set my foot in Mberengwa again. They claimed it was a "no-go area" for parties other than ZANU(PF). It was clear that rampant intimidation was underway in the area and no one else had access to it.

When I reported this to Nkomo, he advised me to keep out of Mberengwa. He said that Lord Soames and his team would look into it. If Soames's people did, it had no effect.

There were many cases of our youths being severely beaten in Mashonaland, but Nkomo would only tell me to take up the matter with my "muzukuru" – meaning Mugabe. I did, and after he had listened to me he called Ernest Kadungure, whose response was "such incidents occur in an election". In other words, he and Mugabe condoned the use of violence .

In Masvingo Province, we were told of panic-stricken mobs of voters besieging the polling stations on the first day of voting, and forcing the officials to keep them open until everyone had voted. And the days after were quiet. We then learnt that ZANU(PF) fighters had let it be known around the province that the first day of voting was meant for ZANU(PF) voters to cast their ballots, and people voting for other parties were to vote on the following two days. Naturally they knew what would happen to them if they voted on the second or third days.

I was watching the television on 4 March, waiting for the results to be announced. Nxele, Nkomo's chief bodyguard, appeared at my front door at about 8 p.m. He was agitated. "The old man wants to see you ... come now, now, now," he said. I followed him in my car to Nkomo's home in Highfield. There I found Nkomo sitting all by himself, watching the television news. The results were being announced by Eric Pope-Simmonds, the Rhodesian Registrar-General. Nkomo was in a state of shock. All hope was lost. PF ZAPU had won 20 seats, in Matabeland and the Midlands. Muzorewa won three and Mugabe took 57. When the announcement was over, he turned to me. "How can you people leave me alone when the results are so bad? Why weren't you with me?" "I'm sorry," I said. "We didn't know it would be so bad." I apologised for leaving him alone. I said again I was really sorry. Then he asked me, "Is this how the people of Zimbabwe thank me for all the suffering and sacrifices I made from 1957 to this year in order to liberate this country? Is this how they think they should thank me?" I didn't know what to say.

"Old Man," I said. "Elections are something else. They don't necessarily define what people think about you, but what they think about you at that particular time, what they have been told about you at that particular time. They were told that for peace and stability in Zimbabwe, they should vote for ZANU(PF), and they have done that. It doesn't mean that they have forgotten what you did." He was distressed and I felt for him.

But as we sat more people started to arrive. There was Josiah Chinamano, PF ZAPU vice-president, also shocked at the result. They were coming in ones and twos and all saying the same thing, that they didn't think it could have been so bad. But also with us was a young British chap who had sensed Nkomo's needs better than all of us. "Oh, Mr Nkomo, I know how you feel. We didn't expect this." And then he asked, "Do you have somebody in particular you want to speak to right away now?" None of us had thought of this. Nkomo said immediately, "Yes, can I speak to my wife – Mafuyana?" She was in East Germany. Nkomo took her number from his wallet and within a few minutes this young man had got her on the line. He said, "Mr Nkomo, here is Mrs Nkomo to speak to you."

We overheard Mrs Nkomo exulting, "Amhlope!" (Ndebele for 'congratulations'). She went on, "Oh, I'm so happy that we have won. I have already packed, and if there was transport to bring me to Zimbabwe tonight I would have come but I have to wait until tomorrow. Oh, I can't wait."

Nkomo was flabbergasted. "No, no, wait," he said. "You're mistaken – we lost."

"What are you talking about?" she replied. "I understand Smith lost and the Patriotic Front won. Were we not fighting for majority rule? I am congratulating you for majority rule. That's what we got. Didn't we get that?" There was a silence and then Nkomo said, "We did." They spoke between themselves for a while and bade each other goodnight.

Then he smiled. "My wife is amazing," he said. He was suddenly a different Nkomo. He had relaxed immediately. "I am telling her that we lost, ZANU won, and she said, 'that is nothing.' She is interested in the whole picture, not just a part of it." He had been getting all sorts of messages from various people, including his fighters who were now saying, "What do we do? We have lost.

What is our future?" Now the conversation took a different turn. There was someone closer to him than anyone else in his life who was very happy that after so many years the destiny of our country was now in our hands.

A few days later we heard that Mugabe, now the prime minister of Zimbabwe, was proposing a government of national unity between ZANU(PF) and PF ZAPU, and would also include minority parties. In a statement on television and radio, he declared a policy of reconciliation towards his enemies. He surprised everybody, friends and foes alike. I was deeply impressed by his appeal for us to "turn our guns into ploughshares".

PF ZAPU's leadership met with Nkomo to discuss the offer of inclusion in a government of national unity. Nkomo was not keen on it. He thought it would weaken the party. He was convinced that if we joined the government, we would find ourselves agreeing with Mugabe more and more and weakening our own position. He knew he would find it difficult to oppose the government in which he was a member. He feared that he would find himself supporting ZANU(PF) policies. He argued that for PF ZAPU to remain an effective opposition party it should stay out of the government. But most of us said, no, this was the time for nation-building. We had negotiated together as the Patriotic Front. Our armies had fought against a common enemy. It was only fair that we should run the country together. Eventually, those who were of this opinion prevailed. Nkomo eventually saw sense in it and he accepted Mugabe's offer.

7

Ministerial Position

Ministry of Youth, Sport and Recreation

A few days later, Mugabe announced his Cabinet. As we expected, ZANU(PF) controlled most of the ministries, but we could live with that. Nkomo told us of our portfolios. In my case he said it had been decided that I would be deputy minister of Youth, Sport and Recreation under Teurai Ropa Nhongo – her *nom de guerre,* "the one who sheds blood". I had never sat down and spoken with her and I didn't know much about her either. All I knew was that she was much younger than I was, scarcely out of her teens, and with very little education. I told Nkomo to tell the PM that I would not accept my appointment. I hadn't given much thought to it. One is often guided by pride and prejudice. It was probably because she was a woman and very young. I told Nkomo this and he said to me, "Are you sure you don't want it?" I said, "Positive, I don't want it."

A few days later he said, "I have told the PM and the PM says I

Part of the first cabinet of the Republic of Zimbabwe, 1980

Back row: G. Chidyausiku, M. Mahachi, W. Mangwenda, V. Chitepo, S. Mazorodze, C.G. Msipa

Middle row: B. Chidzero, E. Zvogbo, N. Shamuyarira, G. Silundika, J. Mujuru, H. Ushewokunze, D. Norman, S. Mubako. F. Ziyambi, O. Munyaradzi

Front row: C. Muchachi, D. Smith, E. Nkala, E. Tekere, S. Muzenda, R. Mugabe, J. Nkomo. M. Nyagumbo, R. Hove, D. Mutumbuka, E. Mnangagwa should leave the matter between him and you. He will talk to you about it, so for now do nothing." I said, "Fine."

A few days later I was called to State House. Mugabe addressed me as "Sekuru" as he always did, and said, "I understand you don't want this post I am giving you. Tell me why you don't want it."

"You know I have a problem with it. For all I know, this girl could be a pupil in my class."

"Yes, which is true," he said.

"Secondly, she could be my daughter – my sons are older than she is. So you're telling me I should work with her under these conditions?"

"Yes, why not?" He explained that his party had agreed that she should be made minister because she was a member of the ZANU(PF) National Executive and secretary of the party's Women's League. He had decided that I should assist her to run this ministry. Then he said to me, "Sekuru, please don't let me down."

I must say, that did the trick. I didn't want to feel that I was letting him down. He was my friend and I wasn't going to disappoint him. So I accepted it, and I did it wholeheartedly, and believe me, we worked extremely well together.

Teurai Ropa surprised me because she was so respectful to me. I had no reason to complain about her behaviour towards me. I heard other deputy ministers complaining that their ministers were arrogant and treated them like servants. But she and I worked so well together, it was as if we were meant for each other. Within a year we had got to know each other extremely well. We had started a new ministry and it was functioning efficiently. I was very happy with the progress we made that year. Cabinet asked us for a recommendation on a location for major sports events. We zeroed in on the site where the National Sports Stadium is now. They asked us to come up with a name for our national football team. We proposed "The Warriors", and it was accepted.

The days we worked together were wonderful for me. We developed a relationship that has lasted to this day, because it was based on mutual respect, and that is how it is that I continue to respect her. I have continued to follow her development and she has made tremendous progress educationally and has remained herself, composed, respectful and down to earth. She amazes me with her ability to handle pressure and to work hard.

We then moved on to prepare for Independence Day, the day that we had been waiting for. On 18 April, 1980, the Union Jack was lowered in Rufaro Stadium in Harari township and the Zimbabwean flag was hoisted. It was really a moving sight, never to be forgotten. I had named my son Charles Nkululeko (Freedom). He was born on 19 April 1965. There I sat in the podium seeing the Union Jack being lowered and the new Zimbabwe flag being hoisted. I said to myself, "I'm having two celebrations, one on the 18th which is the official day of for our independence, and another on the 19th for Charles Nkululeko."

I was happy that I almost got it right, I was happy that we were now a free people, our country was in our hands. I was happy about the little contribution I had made towards our liberation.

Later that year I accompanied President Canaan Banana to the Golden Jubilee of King Sobhuza II who had ruled Swaziland for 50 years. There were thousands of Swazis and hundreds of VIPs from many countries, and, for the first time, a Zimbabwe delegation.

President Banana and I paid a courtesy call on the King at his palace. During our conversation, I asked him how he had remained in power for 50 years without any problems. He said, first, that you must respect your people, in order that they respect you; second, that you must be loyal to your people, so that they will be loyal to you.

We joined the huge crowds and were entertained the Swazi

way. It was my first time to represent my country abroad and I felt highly honoured.

Ministry of Manpower Planning and Development

In 1981, after a year with Joice Mujuru, I was moved to the Ministry of Manpower Planning and Development, where the Minister, Frederick Shava, welcomed me warmly. The permanent secretary was Dr Herbert Murerwa, whom I knew well as we were both former teachers, and members of RATA. He was a gentleman, a civil servant of distinction and a very amusing man.

Almost immediately I was assigned, with Dr Ibbo Mandaza, then a deputy secretary in the ministry, to carry out a survey of the manpower and skills base in the country.

We drafted a comprehensive questionnaire that was meant to be submitted to all employers, companies and non-corporate organisations. They were asked, among many other things, for the qualifications of top management, their remuneration, details of professionals, the skills of other employees and their race. They were sent to every company in Zimbabwe, in industry, mining, agriculture, construction and commerce.

Disappointingly, much of the private sector wanted nothing to do with it. They insisted that much of the information we wanted was confidential and they saw it as government interference, though we assured them their details would be treated in confidence. Many white businessmen accused us of being "communists" and they were deeply suspicious, even hostile on occasion. They feared that what had happened in government with the replacement of white staff with blacks, would overflow into their businesses.

Eventually the report was completed. Not surprisingly, we found that private sector companies made little attempt to train black employees for senior and professional positions, and preferred to import their skilled staff. Managers were almost exclusively white, and generally the highest positions blacks could aspire to was supervisor, frequently referred to as "bossboy." Managers in every sector were almost exclusively white.

Nevertheless, it provided a blueprint for the development of human resources in Zimbabwe, which became the producer of probably the most skilled work force in Africa. Sadly, many senior personnel have since left for other countries where their skills are snapped up.

The first year of independence had not passed before signs of serious friction between ZANU(PF) and PF ZAPU were showing. ZIPRA guerrillas felt they were being discriminated against in the restructuring of the military forces and denied a fair deal in the new national army. There was a growing number of incidents of ZIPRA men deserting their assembly points to become bandits in the bush. ZANLA and ZIPRA guerrillas were moved into large camps in Chitungwiza township just south of Salisbury and in Entumbane on the outskirts of Bulawayo, in each case almost side-by-side. Before long, they were exchanging fire.

At the same time, Enos Nkala was leading a campaign of vilification againsty PF ZAPU. The desertions accelerated and there were attacks – mounted by what the government described as "dissidents" – on ZANU(PF) officials and white farmers in Matabeleland and the Midlands. At the same time, PF ZAPU was unhappy over being issued only four out of 23 full ministerial seats in the Cabinet.

In January 1982 Mugabe decided to remove Joshua Nkomo, Josiah Chinamano, Joseph Msika and other ministers and deputy ministers from Cabinet. I and Clement Muchachi, the party's organising secretary and the minister of public works, were not affected. When Nkomo heard of the sackings, he phoned me and told me what had happened. He asked me whether I would remain in government if he and the others were removed. I told him that I would think about it.

That same morning I received a call inviting me to meet Mugabe at State House. He was with Deputy Prime Minister Simon Muzenda. Both men were in a very jovial mood and greeted me as if nothing had happened. Then Mugabe disclosed why he had called me.

He said that he was removing Nkomo and others from Cabinet because they were "working with dissidents", and he could not continue to sit in Cabinet with people he did not trust. But he said he wanted me to remain in government.

I told him that I did not have the information he had on Nkomo and the others, and did not know how involved they were in the instability. But, I went on, "I wonder how a man like Josiah Chinamano, who is a man of peace, could be involved, because the activities have been happening in Matebeleland and, as far as I know, Chinamano spends most of his time in Harare." I added: "Knowing him as I do, I can't believe that he could be involved in such violent activities."

Mugabe replied that the problem with Chinamano was that he never questioned Nkomo publicly and so for that reason he felt he should remove him. I told him that I was not aware of any instance where his own deputy, Muzenda, had opposed him publicly. Both the prime minister and Cde Muzenda thought this was funny and they laughed, but they did not answer me. I thought this was hypocritical of them. They just laughed as if to say, "He knows that we are not being honest."

They then told me that Muchachi had offered to resign in sympathy with Nkomo. They asked me if I could speak to him because they wanted him to remain in government. They said they did not have any information that he was connected with dissidents. I assured them that I would speak to him and try to advise him to remain. My view of course was that this was a temporary setback in our efforts to work together with ZANU(PF) and that sooner or later we would come together again.

Back in my office, at around 11 a.m., I immediately tried to get hold of Muchachi – who, like me, was from Midlands Province. His wife, who was related to Nkomo, answered the phone. When I asked to speak to him, she answered very angrily that he was asleep and did not want to be disturbed. I could not understand how a man could be sleeping at that time in the morning. I phoned again later only to be told that Muchachi was still asleep and he did not want to be disturbed. I realised that she did not want me to speak to him, despite the fact that she knew that Muchachi and I were very close friends. Then at one o'clock I was shocked to hear over the radio that Clement Muchachi had resigned to show his solidarity with Nkomo. I phoned him again and this time his wife called him to the phone. I realised it was too late, but all the same I asked why he had resigned. I went on to tell him that in Africa, you don't resign, you wait to be dismissed. If you resign you will be seen as challenging the government and you will be considered an enemy. He said he was aware of that, but on principle he felt that his leader had been wrongfully dismissed and his conscience did not allow him to remain in government. I wished him well.

In accepting the offer by the prime minister to remain in government I asked him, "Under what name do I operate?" He said, "PF ZAPU of course," and I said, "In that case it's okay because I believe we must keep our lines of communication working and that's what I will continue to do."

Ministry of Water Resources and Development

Mugabe soon appointed me Minister of Water Resources and Development, to take over from Joseph Msika, who had just been sacked from the Cabinet. I was happy with the promotion, after two years of working as a deputy minister. I made a public statement explaining that I regretted what had happened but I felt there was need to keep the lines of communication open between the two main parties. I described the expulsion as "a temporary setback". Nkomo wanted me to resign but Chinamano and others urged me to remain. I was also happy to be a full minister, and I found my work interesting and exciting.

Visiting a water-treatment plant in India

I took over the ministry during the severe drought years of 1982/83, which placed on my shoulders the enormous burden of having to provide water to drought-stricken areas. My friend Eddison Zvobgo, then Minister of Local Government, jokingly said those droughts were because the ancestral spirits did not want the water ministry to be headed by a PF ZAPU minister. At the time, there was only one black engineer, Andrew Mpala, in my ministry; he had come from Zambia and was PF ZAPU. Each time I held meetings with my senior officials I found myself the only black person in the room. I was uncomfortable with the situation, but I had to live with it. The drought worsened as time passed and the crisis was raised in Cabinet. The prime minister then instructed me to come up with a 10-year dam construction programme – within the next three weeks.

However, before I joined the water ministry, Edgar Tekere, the Minister of Manpower, Planning and Development then, had fired most of the white engineers from the water resources ministry in order to replace them with young blacks. But he forgot that we had only one black engineer and over 50 white engineers. I then had to insist on permission to recall the white engineers because I could not produce the plan with only one black engineer. I got the go-ahead from the Public Service Commission with Mugabe's backing. I told my permanent secretary, Peter Grizick, to invite the white engineers back, most of whom had more than 20 years experience. They all agreed to return, and I explained to them what Cabinet expected of us.

It was a pleasure to see them working so hard. They had only three weeks in which to produce an enormous, complicated plan, but they didn't see it as an impossible task. They wanted to beat the deadline, and they worked long hours of overtime. We made it in time, and I was very grateful to them.

The plan gave a detailed analysis of how many dams should be constructed and where, which ones were for farming purposes, and which were to supply water in urban areas. It was a thoroughly comprehensive document.

But to my regret, nearly 35 years later, some of these dams are still to be constructed, and others are still under construction. Somewhere along the line the dam construction programme lost its urgency.

Kunzvi Dam, which was an urgent project to supply water to Harare has hardly been started, and Harare's water supplies are in crisis.

Tokwe Mukosi, south of Masvingo and designed to be the country's biggest internal dam for massive irrigation projects, is still stalled on and off for lack of finance, and the Italian construction company keeps on moving its equipment on and off the site according to their payments.

But we did manage to build some of them, three big ones and twice as many medium-sized. The Dutch government pledged to provide funds for the construction of medium-size dams. Their Minister of Overseas Development joined us at the commissioning of Wedza Dam in Mashonaland East and she was so impressed she promised to fund more dams.

On the other hand, the Italian government pledged to do a study of the availability of underground water in the Mguza area of Matabeleland North to see if it could be used to supply Bulawayo. The city's current water supply comes from a poor catchment area east of the city. Big rivers such as Gwai and Shangani are far from the city. The Italian government offered as far back as 1980 to do a feasibility study to determine how much water was needed and how it could be drawn to Bulawayo. Unfortunately the study was not carried out because of the threat of attacks by dissidents. Despite our assurance that the army would guard and protect them, the Italian government said the conditions were unacceptable. We ended up sending their team to Muzarabani in Mashonaland Central.

MPs from Matabeleland asked me to inform parliament of the possibility of bringing water from the Zambezi River to Bulawayo. I explained that before the water could run to Bulawayo, it would have to be pumped up the very high and steep escarpment, and we did not have the power resources to do it. The project was of such enormous dimensions, it would have to be left for future generations. My position has not changed.

I also told them that it would be cheaper to construct dams on rivers – particularly the Gwai and the Shangani – that flow into the Kariba dam, rather than allow the water to reach Kariba and then bring it back. A Chinese company was finally awarded the contract in 2004, but since then it has been stop-start, stop-start as the government kept on running out of money.

Impila dam extended between 2000 and 2005

The dam construction report also included immediate plans to increase the distribution of water resources around the country by sinking boreholes and digging wells. We also provided piped water schemes in rural areas which would be a huge help in shortening the long walks by village women to collect water.

Some of these piped water schemes covered long distances; one of them – in my home area in Zvishavane district – stretched for 14 kilometres. I asked the army commander, General Solomon Mujuru, to supply me with soldiers to dig the trenches and lay the pipes. He was happy to oblige. The soldiers dug the trench in a matter of weeks. They established good relations with the community, and some even ended up getting married to local women.

The scheme is still operating. It has been upgraded to include the supply of water to houses for those who can afford to pay for it, and several villagers now have metered water in their homes. I wanted it in my constituency to see how it would work. My aim was to have a piped water project in every district in the country so that people would see that the new government cared for them, and what a difference it would bring to their lives.

I was criticised by some of my colleagues in Cabinet for using government resources to benefit my relatives, but Mugabe defended me. After the ground-breaking ceremony for the piped water scheme in the Zvishivane district, the general and I travelled back to Harare in his car. We talked about the future of the country, and how we saw it. We even talked of a possible future successor to the prime minister – and this was in 1983. As we were driving the general said to me, "Imagine there's a coup in Zimbabwe. Who do you think would take Mugabe's position?"

I immediately cautioned him: "Your question can lead us into serious trouble; these young men [the driver and Mujuru's aides in the car] who are hearing you may tell others that we are planning a coup." He quickly said, "You are right. Let me rephrase my question. If Mugabe suffered a heart attack, who would take over?"

I said, "Muzenda, being the vice-president of ZANU(PF)." I didn't think it worthwhile or wise to continue this conversation in the circumstances.

I enjoyed my work as Minister of Water Resources and Development, and made many friends wherever we supplied water. People gathered to thank me, women baked cakes and wrote on those cakes, "Water is Life" and I took those cakes to my wife.

The Japanese government had been the first to supply us with drilling rigs for water, and I remember the first borehole being drilled as if it were yesterday. The launch was done in Shurugwi district, under Chief Nhema. We had a piped water scheme there and each time I visit the area people talk about it. A few years ago,

Mugabe said to me, "What happened to your piped water scheme? It was a very good scheme." I replied, "As you said, it was my scheme. When you sacked me, the scheme came to a halt."

8

Dissidents and Gukurahundi

It was during my tenure as Minister of Water Resources that the security situation in Matabeleland and the Midlands worsened seriously. It had escalated from isolated instances of banditry to an insurgency.

The insurgents were former ZIPRA fighters who were bitterly dissatisfied with their exclusion by ZANLA senior officers in the national army, from promotion and acceptance. The government decided to call them "dissidents", although this is a word that means someone who disagrees with a system, rather than one who takes up arms against established authority.

They brought havoc to the western region of the country. They were a serious destabilising factor wherever they operated. Development projects were stopped, schools, clinics, hospitals, dip tanks, government offices and even police stations were abandoned all over Matabeleland. Their targets ranged from government officials and white farmers to foreign tourists, and they created an international incident when they abducted and killed a group of six foreign tourists – two Britons, two Americans and two Australians – on the road to Victoria Falls only 76 kilometres from Bulawayo.

It is not known how many dissidents there were or under whose leadership they operated, although Mugabe blamed the leadership of PF ZAPU, which had already been sacked from Cabinet. The government set up two commissions of inquiry – one under Chief Justice Enock Dumbutshena and another under Simplicius Chihambakwe, a lawyer close to ZANU(PF) – to investigate the causes of the mutiny. Their reports were not made public, so it is not known how serious the reasons were for desertion, or the military operation against them, the effects of which, as we were to learn later, were terrible.

Mugabe's government claimed that they were supported by senior PF ZAPU figures. Joshua Nkomo was eventually forced to flee the country for his life under cover of darkness into Botswana on 7 March, 1983 after Mugabe declared at a rally in the Midlands that "ZAPU and its leader, Joshua Nkomo, are like a cobra in the house, and the only way to deal with a snake is to strike it and crush its head." He fled to Britain for his safety for the next three years. Jini Ntuta, a PF ZAPU official, was murdered. The government claimed it was by dissidents, but it was widely believed to be by the army.

John Nkomo and I were the last to be sacked from Mugabe's Cabinet, in 1984. We were accused of "supporting dissidents".

The government response to dissidents was to set up what was known as the Fifth Brigade of the Zimbabwe National Army. It was officially part of the country's defence forces, but it was also a special brigade trained by North Koreans to deal with dissidents. Why it was necessary for North Koreans to train this army, only God knows.

The trail of death and terror that the brigade unleashed in Ma-

tabeleland and the Midlands was named Gukurahundi. In Shona
it refers to a whirlwind which leaves nothing behind in its trail.
Innocent men, women and children perished in their thousands.
They were accused of either harbouring dissidents or supporting
them. It turned out to be a massacre of people perceived to be PF
ZAPU supporters. The fact that people were Ndebele-speakers was
regarded as sufficient proof that they were PF ZAPU supporters
and therefore dissident supporters.

It was reported that up to 20,000 people were killed in the
Gukurahundi operation. Mugabe later described this as "a moment of madness". What that means, I don't know. Thirty-three
years after it was launched, Gukurahundi raises more questions
than answers. Some people feel it should not be discussed in the
interest of national security and peace. What happened was chill-
ing and gruesome and still causes strong emotions.

There is compelling need to look into the aftermath of Gukurahundi. How are the survivors coping? Should there not be compensation for the victims? The remaining family members of many
victims are facing problems in securing ID cards and birth certifi-
cates because the parents who would have signed their application
forms were murdered and there is no death certificate.

There are schools that have mass graves in their grounds into
which all the people of the village, killed by the Fifth Brigade,
were thrown in and covered up. Why should children be exposed
to these mass graves? Could there not be a decent burial for those
who were killed?

Gukurahundi was not a day's event or "a moment of madness".
It began in 1981 and continued until 1987 when the unity accord
was signed between PF ZAPU and ZANU(PF).

There were meetings at which the matter was raised in my presence, and Mugabe insisted that the matter be discussed so he could
learn more about what had happened and was still happening.

The question is, why did he not know what was happening, when it was in the media and many human rights organisations and churches were publicly protesting?

In April 1983, Jacob Mudenda approached me to say that the chairmen of all the rural district councils in Matebeleland North were desperate to appeal to the the prime minister over the intolerable cruelty people were suffering.

I agreed, and asked Emmerson Mnangagwa, then Minister for State Security, if he could arrange a meeting with the delegation. Mugabe consented, and the meeting was set for when he was in Bulawayo for the opening of the Trade Fair.

The six district chairmen were very brave to have exposed themselves like this. They must have feared that they were stirring up a viper's nest by making an approach to the prime minister over an issue of such sensitivity. They were Francis Munkombwe of Binga district, Alexus Chiyasa of Hwange, Amos Mkwananzi of Tsholotsho, Nosembi Khumalo of Nkayi-Lupane, Welshman Mabhena of Nkayi and Elijah Mathe of Bubi.

The meeting started at 6 p.m. at State House in Bulwayo. Mnangagwa declared that he would allow it to last for only 30 minutes. He appeared to have been overruled. It went on for five hours. A woman secretary from the prime minister's office was taking notes. I was not present, but one of the chairpersons told me that one by one, they spoke in graphic detail of the atrocities, and the excessive use of force by the Fifth Brigade against innocent civilians – men, women and children – who were regarded as sympathisers of the insurgents. They detailed the breakdown of civilian administration caused by the military. They implored the prime minister to replace the Fifth Brigade with the Support Unit of the Zimbabwe Republic Police, known as the "Black Boots", who had a reputation as a professional and disciplined force. Mudenda told me that the prime minister then called General Solomon Mujuru to appraise him of the delegation's appeal.

When the meeting ended at 11 p.m., Mugabe invited the district chairpersons to join him for a late dinner. I was given to understand that Mugabe had agreed to the chairpersons' request for the Support Unit to replace the Fifth Brigade, although its deployment was painfully slow. Mudenda stayed in touch with me for months after the meeting, and reported to me later that there had been "a noticeable reduction" in the incidence of Fifth Brigade atrocities.

But of major importance was the request that the chairpersons made to Mugabe that ZANU(PF) and PF ZAPU should engage each other and end the conflict that was costing the lives of thousands. It was here that the first seeds of unity between the two parties were sown.

But Mugabe's promises did not bear fruit. A year later, he said he couldn't understand why people in Matabeleland and the Midlands were continuing to supporting "dissidents." In 1984, he suggested that I, as Minister of Water Resources, and Dzingai Mutumbuka, the Minister of Education, prepare a week-long programme for him to travel around Matabeleland and see what our two ministries had achieved in providing water and building schools in the region. He wanted to demonstrate that the government had not forgotten about the people of Matabeleland.

One morning during the trip, Mnangagwa and I were having breakfast at the Bulawayo Sun hotel when we were surprised to receive a visit from Amos Mkwananzi and Welshman Mabhena, both members of the central committee of PF ZAPU and former detainees under Ian Smith's government. They were outspoken critics of Mugabe's government and were leaders in their own right in Matebeleland, and had been part of the delegation who met Mugabe in Bulawayo the previous year.

They told us they wanted to meet Mugabe again, to draw his

attention to the continuing atrocities still being carried out by the Fifth Brigade in Matebeleland. Mnangagwa said to me: "The prime minister is in Matabeleland to see what your ministries are doing, therefore you are hosting the PM." He said I should convey the request to Mugabe, and promised he would support me.

I did not know how Mugabe would react but all the same I resolved to tell him. To my surprise, he welcomed it without question. He said, "Yes, I want to see them but not just two people. Tell them to bring as many people as they can because I want to know what is happening here in Matabeleland." He gave Mabhena and Mkwananzi two days to organise a meeting at State House in Bulawayo. He would be prepared to hear from people who had first-hand information on what was happening. I conveyed the message to Mkwananzi and Mabhena. They too were pleased at the PM's response.

Come the day, at 2.30 p.m., people filled State House. It was as if a rally had been called. They came on bicycles, in cars, on foot. They wanted to tell the prime minister in their own words what was happening. It was for them a unique opportunity and I felt honoured to chair the meeting. The atmosphere was tense, you could feel it. The people looked angry and bitter. The prime minister was seated on my right side and I first called Mkwananzi and Mabhena and they were very candid. They spoke fluently, with feeling, and minced no words as they described the violence perpetrated by the army. Then I opened the discussion to the gathering and people raised their hands to speak. They spoke, some with tears running down their cheeks, saying how many relatives they had lost at the hands of the soldiers, and how their friends were detained for no reason, tortured, and executed. On and on and on, and the prime minister sat there listening.

For almost two hours, speaker after speaker related events as they had been experienced. When everyone who wanted to, had spoken, I turned to Mugabe and said, "Can you respond please?" You could see that the audience was waiting anxiously to hear what he would say. Everybody was quiet as he stood up to speak. Some thought he was going to defend the actions of the army. To our surprise, he expressed sincere sympathy to the people there for what was taking place in Matebeleland. He assured them that he would do everything to see that peace was restored. He spoke for barely five minutes. He assured the crowd that he would see to it that the brutality would be stopped. I could see people's expressions changing. They were pleased and surprised. Mugabe said, "I am sorry to hear what has been happening and I wanted to assure you that my government will do everything to ensure that there is peace in this part of the country." He added: "I also want to appeal to you to desist from supporting dissidents." People appeared convinced that peace would prevail, and so I closed the meeting.

The outlook suddenly seemed different. People appeared to feel that the prime minister was on their side and sympathetic to their appeals. Mugabe did a convincing job. He did not attempt to justify whatever was happening, or to defend the actions of his soldiers. More impressive was that he remained calm throughout and answered the people in a very respectable and dignified manner and so people returned to wherever they had come from with the expectation that something positive would follow.

I was also flattered; I got some praise for ensuring that the meeting took place and that the people had the rare opportunity to speak directly to the head of government, and that they had heard the assurance they needed. They called me "Umlamula nkunzi", meaning "one who separates bulls that are fighting".

The feedback I got was that from that day there was a lull. Life in Matabeleland appeared to be returning to normal. The killings were reportedly diminishing. The undeclared war caused horrific suffering to a whole people. We had heard reports of whole villages being buried alive. It was impossible to obtain a reliable estimate, but researchers later estimated that as many as 20,000 people died as a result of *Gukurahundi*.

The dissidents were very few indeed, in a staggering disproportion to the number of people who were killed. It took quite some time to bring to a complete end, in 1987, and I have no explanation for why it took so long. People began after a while to feel that peace was coming back to their areas, but what a loss as a result of what Mugabe later called "a moment of madness".

But later on, after the Bulawayo meeting, I witnessed an incident in which my mother-in-law and father-in-law in Insukamini in Lower Gweru were harassed and traumatised and placed under house arrest for two days by a group of violent young men. They were not in uniform but they claimed to be representing the government. They were looking for supporters of PF ZAPU and because I was PF ZAPU I was associated with dissidents, they said. They claimed people were taking advantage of what *Gukurahundi* had done to commit crimes in the name of the army. Having heard the prime minister assuring the people what he was doing to restore peace, I was very angry to see people still being treated in such a manner.

The young men interrogated the villagers on their relations with me and took away the groceries I had given my parents-in-law. They were told they were under house arrest and in future if they allowed me to visit them they would be killed. I was still a minister then. I was enraged.

I raised the incident in Cabinet in a very provocative manner. The people of Matabeleland were being massascred. I was angry and didn't expect a genuine reply from Mugabe. I said, "I find it embarrassing to sit with you in Cabinet when you are busy killing our people." I felt embarrassed because our supporters could not understand why we were in a government that was committing serious atrocities.

Again to my surprise, Mugabe said, "The matter you are raising is very important, and because it's very important, we can't discuss it today." He told me that he would give me all the time I wanted at the Cabinet meeting the following week. "You have to decide how you want to present the case and what you want to say."

I was relieved at the offer. For the next week I carried out research in Matabeleland and the Midlands, talking to friends, to find out what had been happening.

At the Cabinet meeting on the next Tuesday, the prime minister told his ministers that this was a special meeting and that he was giving me the floor to speak. He ordered them not to interrupt me. It was the first time this matter had been raised in Cabinet, and because of its controversial nature, he wanted to ensure that there would be no interruptions. He told them to write down the questions they wanted to ask after I had presented my case.

I spoke freely for about an hour, without any interruption from anybody. I brought with me a list of incidents, and gave copies to Mugabe. I said everything I thought I had to say and I had all the time to myself. When I had finished, ministers were given the opportunity to question me or make their comments. Some of them were very provocative. Others were constructive. Mugabe listened attentively. At the end, and much like at the meeting in Bulawayo, he said, "This was not the time for accusations or counter-accusations. We should all work to restore order and peace in that part of the country." And so the meeting ended.

I don't know why he didn't enter the discussion. He didn't try to defend the government or deny what had happened. He didn't get angry. It was the same as it had been in the large meeting in Bulawayo. He seems to want to do things by consensus.

I think perhaps he wanted to stop *Gukurahundi*. I don't know at what level of ZANU(PF) the decision was made to create and deploy the Fifth Brigade. Maybe he wanted to provide an opportunity to demonstrate to the party how bad the situation had become so he could get their support in stopping the mess.

On the Friday following the "Gukurahundi" Cabinet meeting, a most unfortunate incident occurred in Beitbridge in Matabeleland South. A ZANU(PF) senator from the area, Moven Ndhlovu, was killed in an attack and the government immediately blamed PF ZAPU. I was secretary-general of the party and fingers were immediately pointed at me. That weekend, Mugabe went to speak at the funeral of Senator Ndlovu in Beitbridge. He was in a rage, you could see it on television and you could hear it in his voice. He then declared that from that day onwards people should regard PF ZAPU as "enemy number one of the people of Zimbabwe".

I was watching him on the news on television with my friend Willie Musarurwa at his farm near Harare. I was shocked, but I knew that Mugabe used such occasions to attack his enemies. On this occasion he must have realised later that what he had said would affect my and John Nkomo's positions in government. We wondered what he would do next. We talked until late and when I got home that night, my wife said she had received a message from the PM's secretary telling me to be at his office the following morning at 8.30. I said to my wife, "What does he want from me that he should phone home at night?" She replied: "You're going to be fired." She said it with complete confidence, as if she had been told what was going to happen. She said she could tell from the angry tone of the call that vigorous action was about to be taken.

Indeed she was right.

I got to Mhunumutapa building to find John Nkomo, the only other PF ZAPU minister left in government, there as well. Mugabe and deputy prime minister Simon Muzenda were waiting for us. We sat down facing them and were handed letters in which we were told that our services were no longer required in government.

For my part, while I lost my position as a minister, I am pleased that I had the chance to do three things:

* I made it possible for all the rural district council chairmen in Matebeleland North, led by Advocate Jacob Mudenda in his capacity as provincial administrator, to meet with Mugabe, where they told him of what was happening.

* I chaired a meeting at which Mugabe listened to firsthand information from ordinary people who had witnessed some of the atrocities which were committed.

* I caused the question of Gukurahundi to be discussed in Cabinet after I had raised it. Mugabe responded by saying the matter was so important that it should be discussed at Cabinet.

PM SACKS TWO ZAPU MINISTERS

The Herald 13 November 1984

Mugabe explained why he had taken the action, but he was looking down the whole time, and not at us. I was angry, not so much because I had been dismissed, although the dismissal was a shock to me, but because I had nothing to do with dissidents. My conscience was clear.

Mugabe claimed that we were being dismissed because we gave the impression that we were working together with the rest of the Cabinet when in fact we were secretly supporting dissidents. I was flabbergasted. I told him that the allegations were unfair. He tried to defuse the tension by giving me a general invitation to call on him at State House. We left having been stripped of whatever influence we had as ministers. We were now ordinary men, and everything that came with being a minister – such as bodyguards – was gone. A few hours later, people from the PM's office came to take back my official vehicle. I told them I needed it to take me back to my house.

When the permanent secretary and other members of staff at the Ministry of Water Resources heard of my dismissal, they quickly organised a meeting, collected money and bought me a present and thanked me for the time we had worked together. Later they were questioned about why they had given a present to "a dissident supporter" and the poor chaps explained that as far as they were concerned they had worked very well with me, and what they did was a gesture of appreciation. I then made arrangements to hand back the Mercedes Benz. Fortunately, I had bought my own car a few months before, so I was not stranded. But I really felt humiliated, being treated as if I was a criminal. After my dismissal, the only minister who came to express his dismay was Dr Eddison Zvobgo.

To make matters worse, my driver, Sydney Ncube, and my aide, Jackson Mangisi, were taken to Harare Central police station where they were detained for a week. The Special Branch wanted to find out about what they thought was my involvement in the murder of the senator. They claimed that they had information that I had provided the gun which was used to shoot Moven Ndlovu. Fortunately, Sydney kept a diary and he had made a point of writing down every detail of places we had been to. He handed them the diary and he asked them to see if we had ever been to Beitbridge. That saved them. The truth of the matter was that I had not been to Beitbridge, and my driver had never driven me to Beitbridge. I am made to understand that when Mugabe heard that they were being accused and was told that I was involved in the murder of the senator he said to them, "Look, there are certain things I can believe about Msipa, but when it comes to what you are saying, I can never believe it. He is not a violent man and he cannot be involved in violence." Soon after that, Sydney and Jackson were released. I was relieved to hear neither of them had been assaulted.

A few weeks later I got the shock of my life when five young men arrived at my house one afternoon. My wife and I were relaxing as any wife and husband do during a hot day. The leader of the group told me he was from the CIO and had instructions to search me for arms of war and subversive literature. I looked at him in disbelief. "Young man, you are in the position you now hold because some of us were prepared to suffer and sacrifice our freedom. The prime minister is where he is because we were prepared to suffer and sacrifice. What you are doing is a big insult and I take exception to it." He seemed to have realised how angry I was. He asked to use my phone and I could hear him asking his boss if he had sent him to the right place. His boss must have ordered him to go on with the search. He and his team carried it out, but did it without much enthusiasm. He then reported to me that they had found nothing.

I then asked him, "Can you imagine me and my wife arming ourselves to fight Mugabe's army? Does it make sense?" It made little difference. He said, "We are taking you to the main charge office. Our boss would like to have a word with you." Could I follow them in my car? He politely replied, "It's safer to go in our car."

At the charge office, they handed me over to their boss whom I had known in the Rhodesian days. He also recognised me. He told me that he was serving me with a detention order. Angrily I said to him, "You must be joking! You served me with a detention order during the Smith Regime, the Muzorewa Regime and you think you can do the same under Prime Minister Mugabe now?" I told him I would not look at the detention order and I refused to co-operate with him in any way. I told him that he would have to carry me to wherever they wanted to detain me. It appeared that he was not expecting such resistance. Before he could answer me I ordered him to give me the telephone. I said I wanted to speak to the prime minister. He appeared worried and asked if I had the PM's telephone number. I told him that I did and he allowed me to call. Fortunately Mugabe answered and I briefed him on what had happened. He told me to put the policeman on the line and ordered him to take me back home immediately.

As we were driving back the officer was very friendly and I asked him, "Why did you people want to detain me?" His reply was that when they searched Nkomo's house they came across a letter in which I had asked Nkomo what he knew about dissidents. That was all.

When I got home, I found my friends Willie Musarurwa and Ariston Chambati consoling Charlotte. There was joy and laughter when I told them how I handled the situation. It was a narrow escape from detention by my own government.

But despite our merriment, the incident pained me. To find myself as a political target made me very emotional and very angry.

And now I found myself unemployed again. I had been fired before as a teacher by the Rhodesian government, and by several white-owned companies I worked for, but I did not expect the government I had strived to bring about and longed for, to fire me.

Interestingly, Nkomo advised me to accept it all as it was, and look to the future. I took his advice and quickly adjusted to the new situation and we got on with making our lives.

The "marriage" between PF ZAPU and ZANU(PF) had come

to an end. For Nkomo, it was hell on earth. He was persecuted mercilessly and he eventually had to slip secretly into Botswana, crossing the border in a Land Rover at a deserted stretch in March, 1983. He lived in exile in Britain before the situation allowed him to come back in 1986, on Mugabe's terms.

It wasn't just Joshua Nkomo who underwent shocking treatment. His wife, Johana Mafuyana, was placed under house arrest. Shortly before I was sacked, I visited her at their house in Mpopoma in Bulawayo. There were two woman police officers sitting on either side of her. It was really "house arrest". They were following her everywhere she went, even to the toilet! I couldn't believe what I was seeing. When I returned to Harare I told Enos Nkala – then Minister of Home Affairs – who loathed Nkomo, what I had seen. But even he could not believe it. He suggested I take him to Bulawayo to see for himself. We soon met again at Nkomo's house and he was shocked. He knew of her broadminded and joyous reaction to the results of the 1980 election when she had welcomed ZANU(PF)'s victory because black majority rule had become a reality. I asked myself, "Can she still say that when she is experiencing these horrible conditions?" Nkala said he was furious at what he had seen, and had decided to raise the issue in Cabinet. He told me not to speak in Cabinet on the matter, but to leave it to him. He did. You could hear the rage in his voice and see it in his eyes. The house arrest was lifted and Mrs Nkomo lived a normal life. We were all very pleased that Nkala had done it.

9

The Road to the Unity Accord

The years 1980-84 brought mixed fortunes. At the beginning we celebrated our independence as members of the Patriotic Front. We were together in government, but as time went on we became bitter enemies, to such an extent that the Government of National Unity collapsed. It was a sad ending to something that had started very well.

For a time after my dismissal, Charlotte and I were objects of sympathy. I had no source of income. My wife was the breadwinner from her income as a teacher. We were poor but we were alive.

I had lost jobs before, so I quickly rehabilitated myself. She had also come to accept the situation as part of life. She stood by me in spite of everything against us.

Nkomo returned to Zimbabwe in 1986 and stayed at his other home in Bulawayo, in Pelandaba. He was briefed on the suggestion of talks made at the district council chairpersons' meeting with Mugabe in April 1983, when they said all the enmity and violence would end only when the two parties united. He also held a discussion with Mudenda. He was an excellent person to act as a mediator. He was a provincial administrator and highly respected. I knew him as a teacher and had worked with him when he was a district administrator. He was well liked by those who worked with him and he was apolitical.

Nkomo was very interested in Mudenda's suggestion to explore unity between PF ZAPU and ZANU(PF). He agreed that a go-between should be used between he and Mugabe. They agreed to approach President Canaan Banana, the titular head of state, who was also an Ndebele, but a member of ZANU(PF), and asked him to mediate. Banana, in turn, asked me to assist as another mediator.

***

In September, 1987, my third year year out of government, I was invited to State House in Harare by Rev. Banana. At the time, I was at a board meeting at Triangle Sugar Estate in Chiredzi District when the Secretary to the President, Clifford Sileya, telephoned me with the invitation.

When we met, Banana explained that Nkomo was very keen to talk to Mugabe about uniting their two parties. Banana had tried very hard to set up a meeting, but without success. He said that he had tried to use intermediaries to bring the two together but Mugabe had hard preconditions. In short, ZANU(PF) saw no need for unity with PF ZAPU. Banana continued, "I have been told that Mugabe and Nkomo are both your friends and that if you can't bring them together, no one can."

I had known the two men for a long time and certainly considered both of them my friends. This was at least a good start. I asked what Mugabe was insisting on before he would meet Nkomo.

There were three conditions, he said. The first was that the name of a united party formed between the two would have to be ZANU(PF); second, that the president of the new party would have to be him, Mugabe; and finally there would be two vice-presidents, Joshua Nkomo and Simon Muzenda, who would have equal status.

I told Banana that the first was going to be difficult to sell to Nkomo. Banana said that the way to look it at it was that each party had its own name in it. "You should explain that we have taken ZANU from ZANU(PF), and the PF is from PF ZAPU." I told him we should be honest and say the name will be as it is, ZANU(PF).

I made an appointment to see Nkomo. Although he was not well, he told his secretary to bring me into his bedroom. He was lying on his bed and I sat on a chair next to it. I then explained the purpose of my visit and the conditions for unity as given to me by Banana.

He immediately answered, "These people are not serious about unity. Do they think I can go to Matebeleland and tell people that we are now ZANU(PF?) Don't they know that that name is associated with *Gukurahundi*"?

I suggested to him that we should move to the next two preconditions. He said he had no problem with Mugabe being president of the party after unity but he questioned why Muzenda should be equal to him when he, Nkomo, was leader of the party that was the other partner in the deal. I said that Muzenda would see this as a demotion. I asked him, "Do you see any problem in you being equal to Muzenda?" He shrugged and agreed to it. Then he suggested that we go back to condition number one. He pleaded with me to go and explain to Mugabe personally, and not through Banana. Deep in my heart I knew that if I told Mugabe that Nkomo did not want the name ZANU(PF), he would say, "Nkomo does not want unity." The other issues were not a problem; as I explained to Nkomo, as vice-president he would be in a stronger position to put across his views on any issue.

Nkomo and I had several meetings. I was communicating with

Mugabe through Banana. After each meeting, I wrote a report on the issues raised and Nkomo's responses, to keep Mugabe in the picture. Each time I thought we were making progress, the name ZANU(PF) would occur and take us back to square one. I was on the point of giving up, but Joseph Msika, PF ZAPU vice president, urged me to continue. "This is the most important assignment you have ever been given for your country," he said. Willie Musarurwa and Ariston Chambati were of the same view.

Then I decided to persuade him instead of discussing with him. I appealed to him to give me time to explain to him why I was so anxious for him to unite with Mugabe. Furthermore, I asked him to just take note of what I was going to say and to take time to give it his serious consideration. I said whether it took him a week or a month, I was prepared to wait for his considered final decision. He agreed.

My appeal was in three parts. In the first place, I told him what unity would mean to him personally, that his status would change immediately from being leader of the opposition to being the vice-president of Zimbabwe. Secondly, I referred to the people of Matabeleland in particular – they would feel that they were part of the government of Zimbabwe and that their needs would be attended to at the highest level. Lastly, the country would benefit from his long experience, and policies that were the result of many years of thought, suffering and sacrifice for majority rule in Zimbabwe.

I left him to consider what I had said, and told him I was ready to hear from him whenever he had made up his mind.

Four days later he called me back to ask me if I had discussed the issue with any other members of PF ZAPU. My answer was that I had not (Joseph Msika had asked me not to tell Nkomo of his knowledge of the mediation). Also, during one of my visits to Chikurubi Prison where Dumiso Dabengwa, former ZIPRA head of intelligence, and former ZIPRA commander Lookout Masuku had been in detention without trial for almost a year, I had mentioned the talks. Dabengwa had responded, "How can I give an informed answer to such an important matter when I am isolated from the people?"

Nkomo's initial response was to give me the names of three PF ZAPU people, Welshman Mabena, MP for Matebeleland North, Sydney Malunga, MP for Bulawayo, and Naison Ndhlovu, MP for Matebeleland South. He emphasised that I should talk to them individually about unity between PF ZAPU and ZANU(PF). I arranged to meet each of them and asked them whether they would support unity between PF ZAPU and ZANU(PF) if talks between Nkomo and Mugabe were successful. I was pleasantly surprised when all of them said, "Nkomo is our leader and if he thinks unity with ZANU(PF) is in the best interest of PF ZAPU and the country at large, we shall go along with him." I took the message to Nkomo, who looked at me and said, "Kawungitsheli amanga?" ("Are you not telling lies?").

"I have worked with you for many years," I said. "Have you known me to lie?"

"Go and tell Banana that I have accepted to unite and work with Mugabe," he answered. I could not believe what I was hearing. I was at a loss for words. I thanked him most sincerely and quickly left because I feared that he might change his mind. It seemed too good to be true.

***

As soon as I left Nkomo, I broke the good tidings to Banana who jumped from his seat and congratulated me profusely. His joy is better imagined than described. The following day he called me to say Mugabe wanted him to be given the message from Nkomo himself. Banana asked me to arrange for a meeting with Nkomo. I immediately snapped. "Does Mugabe not believe what I said?"

Banana said, "No, don't be angry, this is normal in agreements like this". I cooled down and passed the message on to Nkomo. He did not appear surprised and we quickly agreed on a date and time when he would come to State House for this historic meeting.

The day came and there was no Nkomo. Banana phoned me from State House to find out where he was. I was in Kariba. I phoned several numbers in Bulawayo and eventually I located him at the Blue Lagoon, a restaurant owned by his daughter, Thandiwe. I asked why he was not in Harare for the appointment and he said he was not feeling well. I asked why he had not phoned to cancel the appointment, and his answer was that his telephone was not working. I was asking in the most polite and friendly manner I could manage under the circumstances. I understood his position. He was consulting close friends. The decision he was making was most difficult. I asked when next he would be able to make the appointment. To my relief, he gave me date and time without any hesitation. I was even more delighted to hear later that he had met Banana as promised. And there my assignment ended. I became a spectator.

No one mentioned my role until long after the Unity Accord of 1987 when Joshua Nkomo invited me to his office in his capacity as vice-president and he said, "Wena mfana ngite ngibong'ukuti wakhuluma lami ngavuma ukuti IPF ZAPU le ZANU sibambane (Young man, I thank you for persuading me to agree to the unity between PF ZAPU and ZANU(PF)). I was not very sure that I had made the right decision. I want to tell you that it is working very well. Thank you for bringing us together." He then asked, "What can we do for you?" I do not know what he had in mind but I said: "By accepting this proposal through me, you have honoured and thanked me." I told him not to worry about me.

I was content that I should not have been given any public recognition. I said to myself, "I have joined thousands who work behind the scenes but are neither mentioned nor recognized." Many people have questioned the benefits of the Unity Accord. I maintain that it was the right decision. It ushered in peace and oneness in Zimbabwe, although some members of PF ZAPU were sceptical.

In April 1988, over 90 dissidents marched to the Zimbabwe Republic Police station at Nkayi in Matebeleland North and asked to see the Governor Jacob Mudenda. They surrendered to him and handed in their weapons. It was immediately after the signing of the Unity Accord. I couldn't think of anything more spectacular and dramatic!

10

Ventures in the Private Sector
and State Enterprises

When I left government at the end of 1984, my friends felt sorry for me. They knew my expulsion was unfair. Nkomo in particular advised me not to show that I was weighed down with problems, as I had no income. He told me to continue to behave as if nothing has happened. "Yes you are down, but you are not beaten." I did try to follow his advice and even went to soccer matches and mixed with people as before.

Then in April 1985 I had an invitation to see David Smith and David Lewis, both prominent businessmen in Zimbabwe. David Smith had been second to Ian Smith in the Rhodesia Front and minister of finance, and had been a moderating influence with the party. We met at Meikles Hotel where I told them that I was disappointed to find myself unemployed because of the actions of people I regarded as my friends. I certainly had had no dealings with dissidents, and it was an accusation that hurt.

We had a chat and they wanted to know what I was doing and how I was surviving. I explained everything to them, basically that having been sacked from government, I now had no source of income and no prospects in sight. Then they said they wanted me to be on the board of Triangle Corporation as a non-executive director. I accepted with delight, and I served on the board from April 1985 to December 1997.

I wasn't the only politically prominent black figure to serve on the board as a director. There was also the respected ZANU(PF) MP, Simba Makoni, who later became Mugabe's minister of finance, and Peter Mahlangu, the secretary of the former Rhodesian African Teachers' Association.

Shortly afterwards, I received many similar offers. I found myself on the boards of Bikita Minerals (lithium mining), Blue Ribbon (milling), Cairns Holdings (food canning), National Merchant Bank (the first black-owned commercial bank), Johnson & Johnson (pharmaceuticals) and Kodak (film). I was attending board meetings almost full-time; it kept me busy and I stopped worrying. It also gave me the opportunity to understand our economy, its challenges and opportunities and many other related issues. In Triangle in particular, I learnt what corporate governance means in business. The company was well run; it was involved in a wide variety of activities, from the growing and processing of sugar, to cotton ginning, ranching, wildlife, and distilling ethanol from sugar cane.

I was deeply impressed with the manner in which David Smith chaired meetings. It was quite remarkable. He showed great leadership qualities, and he used his experience for the good not only of the company but of the country. He was regarded as a moderate, very different from Ian Smith. I grew to see him as a man who was fair and interested in the development of the country and sharing power with black Zimbabweans.

The companies which invited me to join their board of directors wanted to make use of my political background and gain ac-

ces to policy makers. They needed advice to ensure they successfully navigated the changing policy and operating environment.
I also helped to improve communication between government
and the companies that I represented. I visited the USA, with my
wife, Charlotte, as a guest of Kodak and Johnson & Johnson, and
had meetings with external directors of the parent companies.
They wanted my advice on whether there would be any backlash
against them if they continued to do business with South Africa,
where there had been no significant change in the policy of apartheid. Charlotte and I enjoyed the US. Johnson & Johnson treated
me like a VIP, and we were driven everywhere in a limousine.

The Triangle board was very progressive. In 1988, long before the somewhat militant land reform programme, the company launched the first phase of a new scheme to resettle nine new
farmers on 460 hectares of land, of which about 320 hectares was
developed cane land, complete with a homestead, roads, power
lines, irrigation systems and a potable water system. The scheme
was then advertised internally in the company and the applicants
were carefully vetted. The successful applicants had to purchase
their farms over a period of time and were provided with training
and assistance in the first years of their operation.

Mugabe officially opened this scheme at a ceremony at Mpapa
Lodge near Triangle in August 1991. He expressed his appreciation of the scheme and said it was the right thing to do.

The second phase was started in the mid-1990s, adding eight
more farms, each slightly smaller but with the same infrastructure,
and the same selection process. The resettled farmers moved onto
their lands in 1999. The company was waiting for permission to
give the plot holders title deeds but the momentum was lost when
the new land reform policies took over.

The point I am making is that Triangle Sugar Estate was way
ahead of the government in land resettlement. The two pilot

schemes were well received and quite successful.

During my stint in the private sector, I was involved in setting up a local banking institution. Dr Julius Makoni, a chartered accountant, James Mushore and William Nyemba, both career bankers, invited me to become the first chairman of the National Merchant Bank. I told them I knew nothing about banking but they seemed more interested in my name and gravitas. I found myself visiting the boards of insurance and other investment companies to raise seed money.

I was also appointed the first chairman of ZimTrade, a trade promotion organisation set up by the government from levies on foreign trade. I visited many foreign countries. I led a delegation of Zimbabwean business people to the Far East, the first ever by ZimTrade to that region. We visited Singapore, Malaysia, Indonesia and China, all in one trip. In Singapore we were impressed by the technological development we saw, in Malaysia by the level of partnership between the public sector and private sector, while in China we saw the economic giant awakening through what the Chinese called their "open door policy".

During this time, and as Chairman of ZimTrade, I made another visit to the United States of America. Ambassador Amos Midzi organised several meetings around the country. At one of these, I showed illustrations of Zimbabwe that emphasised the mining, manufacturing and tourism sectors. During question time a man in the audience asked, "Were the pictures you showed us from Zimbabwe?" He remained standing after he asked his question, so I knew that he had a follow-up question. When I assured him that everything we had shown was from Zimbabwe he asked, "So why are you poor?"

I replied that the country had potential to develop but that we were not getting enough foreign direct investment. We had the potential, but we weren't able to develop as fast we wanted to, which was why we were mounting such international promotional tours. He sat down.

But that question has haunted me since then. "Why are we poor?" We have a beautiful country endowed with many natural resources. And we are still poor. Our government does not pay much attention to the economy. It spends too much on politics. Its policies don't attract foreign direct investment. They are inconsistent and ambiguous. Take the 51:49 per cent share requirement in the indigenisation policy that became law in 2008. Our attitude is take it or leave it. We are showing little or no interest in foreign direct investment. Generally the message to the outside world is that it is not worth trying to do business in Zimbabwe today. (I am, however, pleased to see that we are now showing an interest in attracting foreign direct investment.)

Added to this is the liquidity crunch, which resulted in money becoming prohibitively expensive and scarce. How do you do business without loans from banks at reasonable interest rates? There is a very serious need for the government to change its economic policies in order to make it a favourable destination for investors.

Thus, it turned out that being sacked from government was a blessing in disguise. I was a free man and I devoted a great deal of time to attending to the boards I served on. It was a huge opportunity to learn more about the country, and about the running of an economy. I realised it was not only the government's job to create economic development, but also the private sector's.

***

In 1985, to my surprise, I was back in government. Moven Mahachi, the Minister of Agriculture, appointed me to the board of the parastatal Agricultural Marketing Authority (AMA), the umbrella body that covered the state-run grain, dairy, cotton, and beef marketing corporations. This could only have been done with the approval of the president, who had sacked me the year before. Mahachi made me vice-chairman of the board. The chairman was Paddy Millar, a very prosperous and efficient white farmer and businessman from Mashonaland Central province, and I had the opportunity to understudy him before I took over from him. I was the first black executive to occupy the position of chairman, and it was a source of great pride to me. Significantly, it enabled me to become very close to government.

Many fellow blacks who were leaders of farmers' organisations, thought the government had made a mistake by appointing me. They said I had no experience in farming so it would be impossible for me to understand the complexities of the agricultural industry; some of them predicted the collapse of the country's sophisticated agricultural industries. So I took my appointment very seriously and was determined to prove them wrong.

The year I served as vice-chairman was enough for me to understand the role of the AMA. In the end I think I performed beyond the expectations of my detractors. I suppose the principles of management are the same whether you are managing a school or a farm. In the years I was chairman, Zimbabwe became known as the breadbasket of southern Africa. Our problem was to find export markets for the big range and volumes of what our farmers produced, which was many times more than the country needed to feed its people. We had meetings with the Maize Board of South Africa, despite the political differences between our two countries, and at one point supplied the whole of the Transvaal province with our maize.

Our coffee grown in the eastern districts was in great demand, and we exported to Europe and Japan, competing with traditional producers like Columbia. We only produced 14,000 tonnes a year, but it was widely sought after as a blend. I had a meeting with Olusegun Obasanjo, the former Nigerian president, who visited Zimbabwe as part of the Eminent Persons Group and wanted to know how the AMA worked. I briefed him, and he seemed to want to introduce our ideas in Nigeria.

Every year we would go to London to raise funds before each marketing season to finance our payment to farmers for their crops and livestock. It was a fascinating experience, meeting representatives of the international banks, and the big British, European, Japanese, Chinese and American finance houses. I would address them and give them estimates of what we were likely to produce and what it would cost. Every year our requirements were over-subscribed. The banks had come to know Zimbabwe over the years and trusted organisations like the AMA. Our credit was good.

We were an important international producer of cotton. It was clean – because it was handpicked rather than machine-harvested – and the fibre was long, so cotton buyers fell over each other to get our crop. We had to have a permanent representative for the board in London – Sylvester Nguni, who later became a government minister.

The Cold Storage Commission also had a London representative, who worked jointly with the Botswana Meat Commission. As Zimbabwean beef was considered among the finest in the world, there was huge demand for it in Europe. Farmers were also producing enormous amounts of milk, so much that the Dairy Marketing Board's facilities were unable to cope with the volume because we didn't have the plant and equipment to process it.

The marketing boards at the time were all headed by whites, except for the Grain Marketing Board, run by Ian Makone, but he resigned in 1988 for a better paid job with Manica Fright (which I joined later as a board member). I recommended his deputy, who was white, to take over from him.

I took his name to Mugabe for confirmation, but he said sharply, "How can you turn our gains into losses? Where there was a black man you are now putting a white man?"

I felt embarrassed. I had thought that the natural thing to do would be to appoint Makone's immediate successor. I apologised and promised to rectify the appointment. Black empowerment was vital to him, but I was looking for continuity and efficiency. I looked around at the managers in the other parastatal boards and the man who impressed me most was Renson Gasela, then the manager of the Cotton Marketing Board. We shifted him to head the GMB and Mugabe was satisfied. After that, one by one, all the marketing boards had black general managers appointed.

It was also a period of dramatic agricultural expansion. We built new grain silos in all the main producing areas to cope with our high production.

Most of the silos you see looming over the landscape today were built in that era of abundant agricultural production, between 1985 and 1995. Most of the funding came from the US government. They were happy with the structure that we had developed for marketing crops and were satisfied that the boards were run efficiently. At that time we still had lots of friends internationally.

Most of those silos are empty now, and run down. We concentrated on redistributing land without giving much thought to the effects on production. The govenment is more concerned with polical interests than economic ones.

In 1992, Zimbabwe suffered its worst drought in living memory. Whole regions had absolutely no rain throughout the season. Cattle were dropping dead in the field, and elephants were collapsing, never to rise again, in national parks. Birds were dropping dead out of the sky. Baboons were raiding villages, they were so desperate. In those areas where there was a little rain, it was barely enough to dampen the ground. Farmers looked up and all they saw was empty blue sky, no clouds, so no rain, nothing. The national harvest crashed.

As chairman of GMB, responsible for providing food for the country, I was very worried. The GMB received the lowest delivery of maize ever, about 45 tonnes compared to the 1 million tonnes in previous years.

Unfortunately, it took much longer for the government to realise how serious the situation was. It was deadly serious. Disaster was looming. We had reached the point where we had about a week's supply of maize. Renson Gasela and I went to South Africa in September 1991 to discuss imports with the South African Maize Board.

While we were there, the Minister of Agriculture, David Karimanzira, ordered us back. He phoned Gasela while were in our meetings with the Maize Board. He said we had no authority to discuss the maize situation in Zimbabwe with South Africa. I decided to ignore him. I said to Gasela, "We will go ahead with discussions and sign an agreement for the purchase of their maize at the price as it now stands." We knew that as soon the grain industry merchants heard that there was an acute shortage of maize in Zimbabwe, they would buy all the available maize in South Africa and sell it to us at a higher price. We had to have the Maize Board sign for the quantity of maize we wanted. If we delayed it would become prohibitively expensive. The Maize Board was very sympathetic to Zimbabwe's looming crisis. But we did not tell them about the problem with our government.

When we returned to Harare, Gasela and I were called to go to the Cabinet office. A special Cabinet Committee had been appointed to interrogate us over our trip to buy maize in South Africa.

I was accused by members of the committee of "causing alarm and despondency" in the country by saying there were no maize stocks. It was a crisis committee at the highest level, chaired by the president and including Vice-President Simon Muzenda, Finance Minister Bernard Chidzero and Agriculture Minister David Karimanzira. Fortunately, I was able to convince them that the situation was dire, that they had to act immediately.

I eventually said to them, "If you don't give us money to buy maize, you people will not be in power because there is no way you can remain in power when people have no food to eat."

Mugabe grasped the severity of the situation before any of the others did, although I had to convince him that his information – supplied by Central Intelligence Organisation (CIO) – that there were stocks of maize in the country was completely false. I challenged him to take me to any grain silo that still had maize in it. He eventually realised that the CIO information was false, and ordered Chidzero to give us the money we wanted immediately. What started as a dramatic meeting where people thought I was going to be fired, ended on a satisfactory note for me because I got what was crucial to avoid disaster. "Thank you for giving us money to buy maize for human consumption," I said. But I hadn't finished. "We also need money for stock feeds." The entire national herd was in danger of being wiped out. My plea was dismissed. The committee thought I was mad to think that money could be spent on stock feeds. Muzenda came to my support and said, "I think what he is saying should be considered. There is no grass, so what are our cattle going to eat?" But they persisted in their refusal. As we were leaving the meeting, I said to Chidzero, "Hey, as Minister of Finance, when you talk about the country's economy, don't you include things like cattle?" He said, "We do." So I said, "Then why didn't you support me, because we are going to lose thousands of cattle, they are going to die." His response was, "I cannot be seen to contradict what the president has said."

I was not surprised to hear that because I know that many ministers are so frightened of Mugabe, they would rather lie to him and pretend things are well than get into trouble for admitting there are problems. My experience is that people do not tell Mugabe the truth, but what they think he wants to hear.

And the cattle did die. They died in their thousands; you could see their carcasses along the roads. So did goats, donkeys, sheep, chickens and every species of wild animal.

I had also asked at the meeting for the right to assume the powers of the Government Tender Board because we wanted to make decisions expeditiously without having to go through drawn-out tender procedures. They also accepted that. I invited the Reserve Bank and the Ministry of Finance to observe the meetings – which I chaired – held to organise the ordering of food supplies.

In deciding who was going to get the tender, we had to consider two factors, the price of commodity and the time it would take to reach us. The situation was so bad that we had to import almost everything edible because there was nothing in the country. Our farmers had grown virtually nothing.

Some foreign organisations were suggesting that supplies should be airlifted. We rejected this because we knew it would be astronomically expensive. We knew that we could do it if we shipped it in using all the ports in Mozambique and in South Africa.

That is what we did. In South Africa, maize was being delivered through Cape Town, Port Elizabeth and Durban. In Mozambique we were receiving our supplies through Beira and Maputo. A constant stream of maize was flowing in daily by road and rail. We averted the disaster which was looming. The GMB's performance was beyond the call of duty. The workers laboured extremely hard and long hours in order to ensure that people did not die, to ensure that the maize was delivered throughout the country, to every district that needed food. It was a huge task but it was done quietly and efficiently so that most people just forgot that we were within a day or two of mass starvation. In fact we ended the year with a big surplus.

There were many people who were highly impressed by what had been done. I remember talking to my mother. She said to me, "You know, that man Mugabe is amazing."

"Why would you say that?" I asked.

"Because he had single-handedly fed the whole nation," she said. "Look at the children. They are looking healthy; they are better fed than when their parents feed them in a normal season. Their parents harvested nothing, but through the efforts of Mugabe, they are looking very healthy."

"How do you think he did it? "

"I don't know," she said. "All I know is that he did it."

"Are you aware that I am the chairman of the Grain Marketing Board and I was in charge of importing all this maize you are talking about?"

"My son," she replied. "In our culture we don't thank the chief's messenger, we thank the chief himself. You were sent by Mugabe so I'm thanking the man who sent you."

I laughed with her but I could see that she really believed in what she was saying. That's what many people thought, particularly in the rural areas. They thought Mugabe was an amazing man.

Then she added, "You know that here in Zvishavane you should never talk ill of Mugabe because people will beat you up."

When I next met Mugabe I told him this story and he laughed and said, "One day you will come with swollen eyes because your mother will have beaten you."

Whatever my mother's feelings in the matter, I was glad that I played an important role in the crisis.

I finished serving the AMA in 1995. I was, however, also appointed to the Natural Resources Board, initially as vice-chairman and then as chairman. I travelled the breadth and length of the country to see conservancies and how they were looking after wildlife and natural resources. My first trip was to the Gwayi area in Matebeleland North and I was greatly impressed. The owners not only protected wildlife and the indigenous vegetation but they built attractive chalets for tourists. I realised that wildlife was a big attraction to tourists. I hadn't known this before. Even now many ministers do not understand how to attract tourists to Africa. One reason is that they have no personal experience and it is not something that gives them votes.

People came from all over the world to visit the conservancies, many of them, all over the country. And I ended up falling in love with wildlife. They looked beautiful. I liked to watch the lions walking, and the huge rhinoceros. They were so rare. And the impalas as they stampeded in large numbers, looking strong and alert. I remembered that in Genesis we read that man was given dominion over everything, but being given dominion did not mean that man was given the right to destroy everything. At school, we had textbooks on the "balance of nature" which taught us that land must be reserved for wildlife and not just human habitation. I became deeply committed to conservation.

I already knew that many of the dams we had constructed were silted up; instead of harnessing water, the pools of clear water in the rivers had dried up because of silt. Rivers which used to flow all year round had become beds of silt, because we had not looked after our soil, grass and trees. I tried to show people that we had a responsibility to look after our resources in our own interest and in the interest of future generations. I addressed meetings and organised competitions in almost every district.

Before I ended my tenure as chairman, we had already started looking at how we could strengthen the Natural Resources Board. We invited experts from other countries to assist us to draft legislation to establish an organisation that would be more effective than the Natural Resources Board was.

As a result of the recommendations, the Environmental Management Agency replaced NRB. But when I see fires in the forests and the grasslands burning, and the dumping of refuse in huge mounds and the indiscriminate destruction of vast swathes of the country, it distresses me greatly. Is it the legislation that is weak or are our people not conscious of the fact that we must look after our resources? Why do we allow the destruction of our environment to take place?

My experience in the private sector and state enterprises was interesting and often exciting. Despite earlier setbacks or disappointments, what mattered to me was that I was working for my country for which I had endured great struggles and sacrifice. It made me very happy to have been able to have contributed to the good of Zimbabwe. I was a happy man. Being of service to our country is what we looked forward to during the struggle. We talked of "the three S's", – suffering, sacrifice and service. We believed that those of us who suffered and sacrificed, would be able to provide service to our country.

11

Returning to Government

In 1994, I was back on the political campaign trail, having succumbed to the entreaties by the chiefs and other influential figures in Zvishavane who wanted me to represent their constituency in parliament. The people of the area responded enthusiastically and voted for me to represent them in parliament in the 1995 elections.

Then, in 1995, President Mugabe called me back into government. He appointed me Minister of State in the President's office responsible for Indigenisation and Privatisation. This was a completely new direction. Before that, the word "indigenous" was not part of our vocabulary. In fact, the title "indigenisation" was the suggestion of Patrick Chinamasa, the attorney-general. We had wanted a ministry of "Black Economic Empowerment" but he advised us that the term "black" had racist connotations. We hoped that if the government chose "indigenisation", it would be more acceptable. The United Nations had made respect and advancement of "indigenous people" an important element of its human rights position. So we zeroed in on "indigenisation".

However, this was a new concept in Zimbabwe and the first

thing we had to do was to explain what it meant. The official intention was to ensure that black Zimbabweans could participate meaningfully in the economy of their country. Much later, in 2005, it was decided it would be achieved by ensuring that all white- or foreign-owned companies had to dispose of 51 per cent of their shareholdings to black Zimbabweans.

We held meetings to explain the idea. At one, the economist Eric Bloch asked me what he would have to do to be accepted as "indigenous". I replied by saying, "If you can marry a second wife and keep the first wife and even go to marry the third wife and keep the other two, then you will qualify as indigenous." I was joking, and I think Mr Bloch understood that I was joking, but there were women lecturers from the University of Zimbabwe who took strong exception and came close to beating me up. They said to my face: "You know, Mr Msipa, we always thought you were a reasonable man but now we can see you are very stupid." They were angry. I tried to explain to them that it was a joke, but they were not amused. I learnt my lesson the hard way about making chauvinist jokes at public meetings. However, I believe that there should have been more discussion about the definition of "indigenous", particularly about the position of, say, third-generation white Zimbabweans.

We invited experts from around the world to help us to understand what indigenisation meant. Dr Carlos Lopes, the UNDP representative in Zimbabwe, brought people who talked about employee stock ownership schemes and indigenisation generally. At one of the meetings Vice-President Muzenda said, "Political power without economic power is meaningless." And it was that message that caught people's attention. People began to think of how they could be involved in the economy. The thinking behind it was that liberation was not just about politics; it was also about equitable distribution of the country's resources. We talked to big companies and told them that it was in their interests to embrace the policy and help us to achieve what we wanted to achieve. We explained that our situation was untenable. We pointed out that in other countries, like Britain, India and Mozambique, their own people were confident they were in control of their economy. But it wasn't like that in Zimbabwe. Black people felt like outsiders in their own country's economy. We could not call ourselves an independent country when we were not in control of the economy.

Some of those companies responded favourably. I remember John Moxon, the chairman of the Meikles group, saying to me he had appointed Much Masunda to the company's board. I told him it wasn't enough, and that he should appoint more blacks to the board, and black managers to his other companies. Anglo American, though, was quick to make advances in indigenisation.

We printed booklets in English, Shona and Ndebele and distributed them in their thousands to help people understand what the concept was all about and why we wanted to indigenise the economy. We received financial support from UNDP and other organisations for workshops and for printing publicity pamphlets.

We had not decided on the legislative framework. We were hoping that white-owned companies would co-operate. The majority did not. I urged the government to enact laws. It was just the beginning. Soon we saw more Africans owning banks, and we were happy about that.

Unfortunately, several of them have collapsed and only a very few have managed to survive and prosper. The Africans who went into banking did not have the capital or the know-how. Some paid themselves high salaries, bought high-end cars and lent money without any caution.

In one sector, we witnessed an immediate transformation. As the state-owned urban bus company began to founder, transport by minibuses became increasingly important. Most of these vehicles, however, were owned by Asian businessmen, often using blacks as frontmen. The ministry set up a facility to help blacks to buy their own minibuses. The change was amazing. Within a short space of time the market was flooded with kombis of all sorts. Unfortunately it has continued to a point where the streets became severely congested. Drivers were easily available and the demand was great.

Cephas Msipa with President Mugabe and Bulawayo Provincial Affairs Minister, Eunice Moyo

During my tenure as the Minister of State, the government also undertook to introduce changes in economic policy that involved reducing state control in the economy and the privatising state-run enterprises. I was able to remove government controls on the marketing of coffee, and from the Dairy Marketing Board and the Cotton Marketing Board.

We privatised the DMB and the CMB by encouraging the new owners to introduce share ownership for their workers, which was also a form of indigenisation. We explained to the workers what it would mean. The point was that every person in the company should feel that it belonged to him or her, and as a result, people would work harder, would be more honest, less inclined to pilfer and would receive many other benefits. All the workers would get their salaries and if a dividend was declared they would get part of it.

Unfortunately, it did not work the way we would have liked it to. The workers preferred to sell their shares to those in management positions. They wanted money, not shares. Most of them were earning below the poverty datum line. The shares had no immediate benefit to them and in any case the concept was new and strange. There was also a fear of company closures. Managers who were better paid took advantage of the lowly-paid to buy their shares from them and ended up benefiting from the dividends.

***

Now I hear that the government is taking back the Cotton Marketing Board, effectively reversing the privatisation we carried out two decades ago. Well, I do not know what we did wrong, if indeed we did.

The adoption of the policy of indigenisation was a big challenge but I am glad that we created an appetite, a desire in the people to run their own businesses and to be employers. Some succeeded and others failed. That's business all over the world. What is important is that we made a new start to our economy.

Interestingly, one of the young people who showed an interest in what I was doing was a young party official named Saviour Kasukuwere. He was based in Mutare but he would attend every meeting I addressed, wherever it was. He showed a great deal of interest and he once took me to his district to show me what the people there were doing, and the remains of what used to be his father's shops in a communal area, until lack of business closed them down. Business had collapsed generally in rural areas and most people shopped in towns.

We also differed sharply with Kasukuwere because he wanted to grab companies in Mutare. I told him, "No, that's not what we are doing, it's not about grabbing companies that are already operating, it's about helping our people to start their own new companies." He then went to the press and insisted that I should resign, because I was "too old". He later apologised for his remarks, and brought a goat to me as a gift.

***

I received a call from the President on 1 August, 2000. We exchanged greetings and he said he had called to ask me if I would accept the position of Governor of the Midlands Province, with immediate effect. I told him that I thought it was wonderful news, something that I had actually been hoping for. I took it as the best way of ending my political career. He laughed. He said he had asked me because Vice-President Muzenda had said I would not accept it, as I had I declined the offer of political office before. In 1990, I was appointed governor then but resigned after 24 hours. I did not like the idea of working under the supervision of Enos Chikowore, the Minister of Local Government with whom I had previously been a fellow Cabinet minister. I felt it was a demotion to have to report to someone who was on the same level as I was, and my friends felt the same. Mugabe accepted my refusal.

So in 2000, when Mugabe's offer for the governorship came again, I accepted. He was delighted.

As we ended our conversation, he said, "By the way, there is a very important meeting tomorrow and that is why I phoned you tonight. It is on the land reform programme, to be addressed by the Vice-President Joseph Msika. Make sure you get details of the meeting."

All the governors, ministers and officials from the Ministry of

Lands had been called to the meeting. Msika explained that land reform was going to be launched. He gave details of its implementation. We were to look for white-owned commercial farms adjacent to communal areas on which to resettle people.

But the overall aim of the new policy was to correct the imbalances of land ownership which had been established by the white minority Rhodesian governments. He said it was now time to act to ensure that "our land comes back to us". The government was not going to pay the farmers for their land, which had been taken from black Zimbabweans without any payment, he said. The British government had promised at the Lancaster House conference to fund land reform on the condition that farms were acquired from white owners on a willing-seller, willing-buyer basis, but they had reneged on the agreement. British Prime Minister Tony Blair had said they were not under any obligation to pay for the wrongs committed during colonial days as they were not involved in the colonisation of Zimbabwe, or words to that effect. Tony Blair's repudiation of Margaret Thatcher's undertaking on land and his imposition of sanctions, together with the European Union and the United States, triggered the farm invasions and all the ills that followed.

The programme would have two categories of settlement: the A1 scheme of small-scale farms for communal people who had no means to buy land but needed it; and the A2 category for would-be black commercial farmers. The sizes of resettlement farms would vary according to rainfall areas. We were told that it was to begin immediately. It was clear that land reform would take centre stage from that day onwards.

I was sworn in as governor back home in the Midlands Province. During the struggle for independence, my father used to ask me, "You are so committed to the struggle, but do you think that when you people take over the country you will have your own piece of land?" I wished he was alive to see me now. I would be operating where I grew up and I would be interacting with people I have known for years, and redistributing land.

In Gweru, the Midlands capital, I met my staff, and the provincial administrator, Martin Rushwaya, whom I knew as a hardworking young man. I was especially pleased to work with him because his mother and my sister were best friends. It was as if I was working with my own son.

We set up a provincial lands committee, which I chaired, and which comprised members from the party, local government and other interested stakeholders. At our first meeting, I instructed officials in the Ministry of Lands to identify farms adjacent to communal areas.

Most of the officials were sceptical, and thought it was the usual government propaganda. They did not believe that it would be implemented as outlined. But once we started, the programme gathered momentum; people came forward waiting to be allocated land.

The first commercial farm we picked was just a few kilometres outside Gweru. We called local chiefs to attend and we conducted traditional rituals so that our ancestors would bless what we were doing and to ensure the programme would proceed without any problems.

The owner of the farm, Rev. Reggie McLean of the Baptist church, had three farms and I told him we were going to take two of them. He astonished me when he said, "You can take all three." Together they comprised over 1,500 hectares. I asked him why and he replied, "You need them to resettle your people." I asked him if he was angry that we were taking the farms, and forcing him to abandon farming. He explained that he had two daughters in the UK who were not interested in coming back to Zimbabwe and he intended to leave the country to join them. This was an opportunity for him to donate the farms. I must say I was pleasantly surprised. We agreed he would have 60 days in which to sell his cattle. He showed them to me. They were beautiful Brahman cattle and included bulls and heifers. Jokingly I said, "Why don't you leave one bull for the incoming settlers? They would remember you by that, and it will improve the quality of their own cattle." He promised to think about it.

Sixty days later he was gone, but he had left the bull behind. It was an excellent start for the land reform programme.

But we did not get the same response again. Some agreed to downsize their farms, and in some areas there was stiff resistance. The white farmers were shocked, and I could understand why. Some of them had been on the farms for many years and they had developed them, not only their farms but their homes as well. We were rendering them homeless. The only life they knew was farming. I really felt sorry for them, but I had to carry out government policy, and to try and do it as fairly as possible.

I decided to acquaint myself with the farms. I wanted to understand the operations of the targeted farms. One of the commercial farmers, Piet de Bruyn, offered to take me around and introduce me to his colleagues. Most of the farms were well developed and highly productive. I could also see that in some cases – for instance, dairy farms – peasant farmers would find it difficult to run them. I invited my Cabinet colleagues from the Midlands, Emmerson Mnangagwa and Richard Hove, to visit some of the farms with me. I knew I would need their support in political discussions. We agreed to spare dairy farms because of their highly technical nature and the considerable finances needed to run them. We announced that they were not to be resettled, and would remain intact in the interest of the country. Sub-dividing them would render them unviable and would not make economic sense. We stuck to that decision throughout the land reform programme in the

Midlands.

Two dairymen, Darren Coetzee and Herman Venter, got approval from the provincial ZANU(PF) leadership to found a new operation, Dendairy, in 2004 in Kwekwe. They started as a very small operation, producing about 1,000 litres of milk a day. The company has since grown and by 2012 it had increased its capacity to one million litres per month. It also increased its product range to include ice cream, flavoured milk and milk powder to replace imports from South Africa.

The new factory was constructed and completed by the end of 2013. With the increased capacity, Dendairy has increased its work force to 210 employees and has subsequently taken on new farmers from Bulawayo and Beatrice to supply its milk. With this new technology Dendairy has been able to increase its product range and shelf-life so that these products can get to the most remote areas as well as to export markets. Other white commercial dairy farmers are encouraging and assisting small scale indigenous farmers to go into dairy production.

Several other white farmers came forward with suggestions and I listened to them and if they made sense to me, I accepted them. One of them, Andy Shaw, said he had three farms; could he offer the government two of them and remain with one dairy farm? I went to see what was happening. Indeed the dairy farm was well run, and, in addition to dairy, he was also running a horticulture operation and cattle ranching. The land was well utilized and I accepted his suggestion.

But despite our agreement, the threat to his life's work had proved a severe shock to him. He realised that change was taking place and that he could not resist it. I was sorry to learn a few months later that he had died of a heart attack. I went to attend his funeral because in that short space of time I had come to like him. I said to myself, can it be that I caused his death? His son took over the farm and I go there from time to time to see if he is still operating. It has since been reduced in size but he is still running the dairy and I am very relieved.

As time went on, more and more people wanted land; some started invading the farms without going through the official process. I wanted to put a human face to the land reform programme and was talking to the white farmers to try and make them understand why we had embarked on it, and that it was necessary to correct the injustices of the past. This was all the result of the Southern Rhodesian government's introduction of the Land Apportionment Act of 1930, which divided the country into separate regions of land for whites and for blacks, and which reserved more land for whites than the blacks. It had resulted in the forced removal of thousands of people from their ancestral homes to completely new areas, some of which were infested with tsetse fly, and unsuitable for human habitation. But as far as the Rhodesian government was concerned, the aim was to make room for whites. After 1930, whites owned more fertile land than blacks, the original inhabitants of that land. In 2000, many Zimbabweans were surprised that it had taken so long for the government to launch the farm seizures, knowing how central the land issue had been in the liberation struggle. The political slogan in the late 1950s and early 1960s was, "one-man, one-vote, freedom now and land to the people!" Now, people were saying, "yes, we are now independent, we are a free people and free to choose our government. But where is the land?" So in 2000, the government decided to answer that question effectively, and launched the land reform programme. People demanded change and were getting impatient. Land ownership was at the core of the war of liberation.

But at the same time, Mugabe was also under heavy political pressure, particularly after the creation of the MDC and the strong support it was getting. Worst of all for Mugabe was the fact that white farmers were openly supporting the MDC. He saw it as a rejection of the policy of reconciliation with whites that he adopted at independence. He felt it gave him justification to seize their farms.

The way we implemented the land reform programme in the Midlands was different from the violent, lawless way it was done in other provinces. We tried as much as we could to carry it out peacefully and so there was no violence at all. On one occasion, three white farmers, Leon Heathcoat, Brian Hein and one Falkensen, were arrested for refusing to vacate their farms in Gweru district. When I heard about it, I spoke to the Attorney-General, Patrick Chinamasa. I told him that I was talking with them and there was no point in the police arresting them. He advised me to speak to the prosecutor in Gweru where they were being held, and ask for their release. I did so, and they were soon free men again. They were relieved that they did not have to spend the night in police cells. Eventually we reached agreement for them to give up part of their farms and the need to arrest them fell away.

Ian Smith, the former prime minister of Rhodesia and the driver behind the illegal independence of Rhodesia, was the owner of Gwenoro farm, not far from Gweru. I told my lands officials, "Can you go there and leave him with slightly over 500 hectares?" I knew he had cattle; he was a good rancher and his animals won prizes. He also had an extensive and high-quality orange orchard, and the fruit was very popular, particularly with vendors in Gweru and Shurugwi. He was born on Gwenoro, and his father had had a butchery in Shurugwi. He had been a student at Chaplin High School in Gweru where he won the first prize in four successive years in sports. It is said he used to steal meat from his father's butchery to give to the children of the farm's workers, who included Josiah Tongogara. Some of his workers were born on the farm and their children are still there. Smith was now well into his seventies.

When the officials from the Ministry of Lands told him that the government was taking part of his farm he could not believe it. He phoned me. He was angry and bitter. I asked if he was at the farm and he said, yes. Immediately I drove to Gwenoro and I asked him what the problem was. He told me of the arrival of the lands officials and asked why we were taking away the farm.

I looked at him and said, "Do you remember when you called me to your office in Salisbury while the Lancaster House talks were dragging on?"

He looked at me, trying to recall the incident. "Yes."

"You asked me then, 'Why is the Patriotic Front talking to the British about land? Tell Nkomo and Mugabe to come back and run this country, they should not allow the British to make laws for them'". He had gone further to say the land problem was for the people of Zimbabwe, for the government-in-waiting.

He looked at me and smiled, as if to say, 'You've caught me.' I thought it was a very gentlemanly acknowledgment.

I had then asked him, "What if the PF lose the election?" to which he had responded: "I have surrendered, and Bishop Muzorewa is finished, so who else can win that election except the Patriotic Front?" Once the PF were in power, he said then, they would introduce new laws.

Now I said to him, "We have won the election and we have been running the country since 1980. We have made the laws concerning the ownership of the land and this is what we are implementing now, so what is the problem?"

He smiled. "But you should be reasonable about it." I told him that was why we were leaving him with the most productive part of his farm, his orange orchard. He had no choice but to accept the situation. From that day onwards he had my mobile telephone number, and if there was any problem, he would phone me and we would sort it out. Mugabe did not know about this arrangement. I doubt if he would have been happy with it.

Up until Smith's death in 2007, he still owned half of his farm, the other half was taken for resettlement. But shortly before he died in Cape Town, I suggested to Mugabe that Smith's half of Gwenoro should be given to the Midlands State University (MSU) for agricultural research and training.

Mugabe instantly become angry. He demanded to know why Smith's children weren't being allowed to inherit it. "Why do you want to take his farm?" he charged. I explained that there had been no expression of interest from the children, and it could be well used by the university. But Mugabe was adamant. I was surprised at his reaction. I would have thought he hated Smith. For my part, I just didn't think he should be given special treatment.

Mugabe, however, changed his mind in 2009. Smith's half of the farm was donated to MSU. The university has maintained the operations, kept the manager and all the workers, and the cattle are in good condition, just as if Ian Smith was still there.

Then there was the case of Phillip Hapelt, whose wife phoned to ask me to come and see her husband. She said he was in shock and was near to death. I went there immediately. He had been born on his farm, he had a beautiful house, and was now about eighty years old. He could not understand what was happening. He had allowed the government to take seven of his eight farms. But a group of invaders had come to take the last one and it was a severe blow to him. I assured him that we would order the invaders off, and that their action was wrong. Eventually, he recovered from the shock and all seemed well. My plan was that Mr Hapelt be allowed to remain on his farm and the house could be turned into a community centre after he had died.

Unfortunately, after I retired as governor, his farm was taken away and he left Gweru for Bulawayo where he had to end his life in an old people's home. I really felt that was a tragic mistake.

From the beginning of the land campaign I had wanted to place an age limit protecting the properties of owners who were over 75 years old. It is unreasonable to expect that people at that age should start a new life again. I really felt sorry for them. But such provisions were not included in the regulations.

There were people who owned vast farms. One of them, Nicholas van Hoogstraten, a man with a rather controversial reputation, who moved to Zimbabwe after 2000 and was a vocal supporter of ZANU(PF), took me on a tour of his property, Central Estates in Mvuma, which covered 123,000 hectares. He had undertaken big developments, building dams, a school, a clinic (named after Simon Muzenda, who came from the district) and staff houses. He was in the process of building a two-storey house for himself. The farm was big enough to accommodate thousands of people but he owned it alone. He drove me around it, until we came to a place where he realised he was lost. He had to phone the farm manager to find out where we were. The situation was unsustainable.

Some of the farmers were unreasonable, and refused to co-operate with us because they thought the British government would stop the programme. Others were confident that at some point they would be paid compensation for the loss of their farms, so they held on to their title deeds and refused to co-operate. I could not do anything in such cases. Eventually they lost out. Some of them came back to me later and I told them they had resisted my offers. They wanted me to negotiate terms for their exit, but by then they had been given orders of eviction. It seemed it was out of my hands.

The events of the time made me think of Benjamin Burombo and his campaign in the fifties against the Land Apportionment Act and the removal of black people from their homes in order to create space for white settlers. He had hoped against hope that the whole exercise would be reversed but his cry was a voice in the wilderness, and no one paid any attention. I wished he was alive now, so he he could see that the evil he had fought against had been destroyed. I feel sure that he would have supported the land reform programme, but not the violence that characterised it in the rest of the country.

***

My adoptive grandmother, Tazviripa Moyo, lived in Insiza District in Matabeleland South, about 70 kilometres from Zvishavane, where I was born.There was no transport and so it seemed to us that she and her family lived in a foreign country. Every year, I used to visit her with my mother. We walked all the way, two days there and two days back. I loved it; it was a joy to see my grandmother and to tell other schoolboys what I had done during the school holidays.

Then one year we stopped going. I asked my mother what had happened. She said my grandmother had been removed from Insiza and taken to some place that she – my grandmother – did not know. Government workers, including policemen and messengers, in the Insiza area heard that lorries had come and transported the belongings of my grandmother's village to a new place. We did not know where it was; all we knew was that Insiza was now meant for white farmers under the Land Apportionment Act.

Two years later she arrived unexpectedly and she told us that she was now living at a place called Kana in the remote north of the country. She narrated her ordeal. She said lorries had arrived without notice, their belongings were loaded up and they were ordered to climb on as well. Their cattle were sold at a set price, and they were driven to Kana, which was a wild, undeveloped place.

Their lives were disrupted; they were not treated as human beings should be treated. They were treated like furniture. Worse

– in the case of furniture, care is taken not to damage it, but in the case of the eviction of people then, a lot of harm was done emotionally and otherwise. A great deal of suffering was inflicted on the people just because they were black.

Yet it was a wonderful reunion. The anxiety which we had felt disappeared. We then knew where she was and how to get there.

But it still makes me angry to think how people were uprooted from their homes then.

I think the Western countries that criticised the land reform programme have not cared enough to find out how we lost our land in the first place. The re-ingagement that seems now to be gathering momentum between Zimbabwe, the European Union and the UK should create an opportunity for all the parties to reflect on the land reform, and its impact on former farm workers, former white commercial farmers, and the country's agricultural productivity in general. Let us all look at the exercise as an opportunity to improve the livelihood of the majority of our people.

I have hoped the international community would say the land reform programme was done and it is over, perhaps now we must look for a way of reconstruction.

Land has been a critical issue from the day Cecil John Rhodes' Pioneer Column annexed the country. The name Rhodesia itself was a constant reminder that we could not belong to the land we and our forebears were born on. The past is history; it is irreversible, and so is land reform. It was the biggest campaign of social readjustment and restitution ever undertaken in the country. It had to be done for sustainable development and stability. The problems of skewed land ownership in the country desperately needed to be attended to. The inequities persisted for 20 years after independence. Many people were surprised that Mugabe had waited so long.

Major errors were made, but in a programme of such gigantic

proportions, that was to be expected. Most evicted white farmers were able to adapt and turn to other ways of making a living, but it was a different story for the estimated 300,000 farm workers who lost their homes and jobs.

One thing which we are to blame for, is that the programme seems to be dragging on and on. Fifteen years down the line, people are still carrying out farm invasions. A halt should have been declared at some point, in order for commercial farmers still with land to concentrate on production and to assure them of security of tenure.

We still have a lot to learn in order to regain our status as the breadbasket of the region. The fact that we have to import maize and wheat from South Africa and Zambia, which suffer similar climatic problems as we do, is an embarrassment.

Some of the new farmers are doing extremely well. But to be successful means working at it full time. White farmers were on the land all the time, 24 hours a day, every day. It was their work, their home and their life. You can't be a telephone farmer.

I became a beneficiary of the land reform programme myself. I did not invade the farm that I'm on, Cheshire farm. The Provincial Lands Committee identified it for resettlement. It had been a dairy farm but the owner, Graham Ingle, had reduced his herd from 200 to 15 and the committee felt that he had lost interest in dairy farming. They asked me to take over the farm and perhaps revive the dairy project. I talked to Ingle and told him that the lands committee had chosen me to take over his farm. He was in his fifties, and we had known each other since my appointment as governor in 2000, when he came to my office, seeking assistance in getting a passport so he could travel to Australia. So he was greatly relieved that it was to be me to take over his farm. I told him that I was prepared to pay him for all the developments that he had built up. We agreed to carry out an evaluation and he looked for an evaluator. It was done and he presented me with a bill. I went to my bank and made arrangements for him to be paid. I also told him that he had an obligation to his former employees, some of whom had been with him for thirty years. With the assistance of the Ministry of Labour, an amount was agreed on for each worker and they were all paid what was considered their gratuity for having worked for him. I turned to the workers and said, "Now that you have been paid, it is up to you to decide whether to leave this farm or to continue with me, but with the clear understanding that you are starting afresh." They agreed to stay.

Except for a few retrenchments, I still have the same workers on my farm. There haven't been any drastic changes at all. My dairy cattle have increased from 15 to around 70 now.

Ingle and I also discussed his future. He told me he was going to live in Australia, and I helped him to have his passport processed. He had a sister living with him who was mentally disabled and he asked me to write to the British government to allow her into the UK so she could be admitted to a home for people with mental disabilities. I did, and fortunately, the British authorities accepted her. I asked him when he intended to leave the farm that had now become mine. He suggested a date and I agreed. He telephoned me not long after this to say he had decided to leave much earlier than he had initially intended, and could I come and occupy the farm almost immediately. I did. I am still in contact with Ingle in Australia, where he is managing a big sheep farm. We still share a warm friendship.

And this is not an isolated case; Emerson Mnangagwa, now a vice-president, made similar arrangements in taking over a farm in Kwekwe District.

An example of how land reform should not be carried out was demonstrated after I resigned from my governorship in 2008.

Along the Sebakwe River in the Midlands, commercial farmers

had established the Sebakwe Conservancies, about 40 sanctuaries for wildlife that attracted a significant number of tourists to the province, provided employment for hundreds of people and looked after the area's wildlife.

But after I left, it was decided to hand them over for resettlement. The new settlers did not know that they had been placed there to take care of the wildlife. They did not know they had to spend money on employing security guards to prevent poaching. It did not mean they could kill the animals. But that is precisely what our new farmers did in the Sebakwe conservancies. They are now white elephants, all of them, with no wildlife. The chalets that had been constructed are falling apart and there have been no visitors there for years. Even the people who had been allocated the conservancies have abandoned them. The problem was in the choice of beneficiaries. Party officials were given the conservancies, regardless of their ability to sustain them. As I write, they are all deserted. I think we are to blame by failing to make the right choice of people to be resettled there, and in the process we destroyed what was an excellent attraction for tourists to the Midlands that could have been of immense benefit to the settlers and to the province's economy.

The only wildlife sanctuary now left in the Midlands is Antelope Park, just outside Gweru, a very popular resort where tourists can go walking with lions and have a ride on one of its many elephants. It employs over 150 people, and at any one time over 20 local interns from Zimbabwe's educational institutions are getting an introduction to the tourism industry.

The owner, Andrew Connolly, a third-generation white Zimbabwean, has built an education centre where 1,500 school children have been taught the importance of wildlife and protecting its habitat. The company has taken conservation education directly to schools in Gweru. The African Lion and Environmental Research Trust (ALERT), based on the park, is one of Africa's and the world's foremost lion conservation organisations and has pioneered strategies to conserve lion populations for generations to come. A few ministers who have visited the resort have shown some appreciation for what he is doing.

The other conservancies are all gone. They are casualties of the land reform programme. We should have treated them in the same manner we treated dairy farmers. Now is the time to concentrate on using the land productively.

Operation Murambatsvina – restore order

In 2005 the president and his officials carried out a nationwide operation that sharply contradicted the government's stand of caring for the homes and security of ordinary people.

"Operation Restore Order" (sweep out the filth), also called *Murambatsvina*, brought about the destruction of the homes of people all over the country, with the displacement of some 700,000 families. It attracted criticism from within and outside the country. The official reasons given for the operation included the crackdown on illegal housing and commercial activities and an effort to reduce the spread of infectious diseases in these areas.

The demolition was ruthlessly done in the glare of TV and other media. Knowing Mugabe as I did, I could not believe that he had authorised such an operation. So I phoned him and asked why it was being done. I remember telling him, "People are asking me why the president has turned against us, what wrong have we done?"

He replied that there was a need to clean up slum areas and to demolish illegal housing and commercial activities.

I then turned to Chombo, the Local Government minister, who said the aim was to encourage people to build decent accommodation for themselves. He assured me that he would make land available for the purpose.

Anna Tibaijuka, the Executive Director of the United Nations Human Settlements Programme, flew in to see what was happening, and travelled all over the country, speaking to people whose homes had been destroyed. Her report was handed to the Zimbabwean government on 21 July, 2005. Excerpts from the report – which called for all demolitions to be stopped immediately – were made public the following day and described the operation as a disastrous venture which had violated international law and led to a serious humanitarian crisis. The actions of the government were described as "indiscriminate, unjustified and conducted without regard of human suffering".

During her visit, Tibaijuka visited Gweru. I drove her around to show her that we were not demolishing people's houses in the Midlands. I also showed her that the vendors were continuing with their business at designated areas. She was greatly surprised and she wanted to know how we had avoided the catastrophe which she had seen in Harare, where she had seen bulldozers demolishing houses in her presence.

I told her that I had restrained the police in the Midlands from joining the home-wrecking. It had not been easy to stop them, but I told them that in terms of their orders they were only allowed to destroy "illegal" structures.

The police commissioner commanding Midlands Province pleaded with me: "You want me to lose my job?"

"You can tell your Harare office that I stopped you from wantonly demolishing people's houses," I said.

Not only did we avoid demolishing people's homes, we also took advantage of government support to encourage our people to build decent houses. Committees were established in every district and these worked with local authorities and housing co-operatives to identify land and build houses.

The committees included representatives from the local government, the army, the police and people from the private sector. The biggest piece of land given to us by the government was known as Woodlands, in Gweru. I had it divided into two and gave one half to the local government ministry, headed by Mrs Agnes Manambo, and the other half to a co-operative led by Mrs Smiley Dube. I explained to them that I wanted to see which system, the private or the public, would produce better results in the housing delivery.

Mrs Dube has since turned her co-operative into a private company, River Valley Properties, and has been awarded prizes at provincial and national level for her contribution to housing construction. These two women have changed the landscape of housing in the Midlands. We can say that instead of being complicit in massive homelessness, we managed to take advantage of Murambabtsvina and inspired our people to build decent houses for themselves.

Today I think I can honestly say that the Midlands is the best province in the country in terms of housing delivery. Some co-operatives have written to the council suggesting that their houses be named "Msipa Park" in appreciation of our attempts to help them own stands on which they have built their own homes.

The Mining Industry and Community Development

While I was Midlands governor, the mining industry showed what a massive role it can play in bringing social and economic development to large centres of population around them.

Three major mines were established in the province while I was governor, all of them on the Great Dyke geological structure around Zvishavane: Mimosa platinum mine, a joint venture between South Africa-based Zimplats and Australia-based Aquarius; Murowa diamond mine, a Rio Tinto subsidiary; and Anglo American's Unki platinum mine They created employment, built houses for their workers and took on social responsibilities.

Mimosa Mining changed the landscape of Zvishavane. When Alexander Mhembere, the CEO of Mimosa for several years, was transferred to Zimplats, and had to move to the company's head office, he telephoned me to ask what he could do to remind the people of Zvishavane how well we had worked together. It was a most unusual request. My immediate question was, "How much are you prepared to spend?"

"The cost is not your problem; just tell me what you want me to do."

I had to think fast. "Could you build a mortuary at the district hospital in Zvishavane?" He agreed. Then I also remembered that the headmistress of Dadaya Primary School had asked me recently for help in building new classroom blocks. I quickly added it to my list.

Both my wishes were accepted and carried out. Zvishavane now boasts a mortuary that can accommodate seventy bodies, compared to the old one which could accommodate only four. Dadaya Primary School was the proud recipient of eight classroom blocks. Both the mortuary and the classroom buildings all had fittings and furniture. It made a very major impression on me.

Mhembere's successor, Winston Chitando, showed the same commitment to the Midlands community. He was involved in establishing a new water supply system at Midlands State University, and the refurbishment of hospitals and hostels, not just in Zvishavane, but also in Harare and Bulawayo. Without Mimosa, Zvishavane would have died. Thanks to Mimosa, the town is not only alive, but continues to grow.

Murowa Diamonds then delivered a shining example of how people should be carefully and respectfully relocated from their homes to make room for mining activities. Rio Tinto directors wanted land for a major new operation but had to resettle 500 families occupying an area targeted for mining at Murowa in

Zvishavane. I showed the mine management, led by John Nixon, the deputy chairman of Rio Tinto, a number of farms in the Midlands. They turned them down, saying they wanted better agricultural land. Finally they came up with a proposal to resettle the affected families at Mashava Mine in Masvingo Province, about 40 km from Murowa. After negotiating with the provincial and national authorities, and getting the assent of Chief Mazvihwa and the villagers, the families were relocated. Rio Tinto provided them with brick-built houses – compared to their former pole and daga homes in Murowa – as well as a church and a school. It tilled the land and provided inputs for the farmers. The families are far better off than those they left behind in Zvishavane district.

Representing the company in all the delicate and intricate negotiations was Israel Chokuwenga, a recognised international expert in the relocation of communities. He had been engaged by Rio Tinto to liase with the Murowa community and other authorities, and is doing similar work in Mozambique .

Finally there was Anglo American's Unki Mine, in the Shurugwi District. The corporation worked with me closely through James Maposa, its non-executive chairman in Zimbabwe. We resettled about 200 families quietly on nearby farms, and they were provided with housing and schools. Shurugwi Town was also dying, but thanks to Unki it is a hive of activity and growing fast.

Before they could start mining operations, a large water supply had to be established, and they pressed me to allow them to construct a huge dam in the Boterekwa hills near Shurugwi. They were getting tangled in red tape in Harare and appealed to me. I tried to resist giving them the permission they needed, as it was a responsibility of the Ministry of Water Resources.

Then one of the directors asked me, "Aren't you appointed to promote development? We can't start mining until we are assured of a water supply." That did the trick. I gave them the go-ahead to

construct the dam and they went ahead with their mining operations. There was no reaction from the ministry. I do not think they
have this in their records.

Like the other mines operating in the area, Anglo is heavily
involved in community development in Shurugwi and Gweru.

When I was campaigning to be elected to parliament in 1980,
I promised the the people in Zvishavane that I would put Zvishavane on the map. I fulfilled that promise as an MP and governor, although in reality it is the people of Zvishavane who put me
on the map. Whatever political success I have achieved is due to
the support I received and continue to receive from the people
in Zvishavane. They don't call me "chef", but "mdara" (old man).
Some are now calling me Father Zvishavane.

How nice of them.

Elections in 2008

After a peaceful campaign period, voting for the presidential and
parliamentary elections took place on 29 March. People waited
and waited for the results, but the Zimbabwe Election Commission announced that there had to be a recount. The MDC and
observer groups objected strongly, but the ZEC went ahead and
organised a recount.

The results were announced on 2 May, five weeks after the
voting had been held. Tsvangirai's MDC won 99 seats and went
into a coalition with Arthur Mutambara's MDC which had ten.
ZANU(PF) got 97 seats.

Tsvangirai won the presidential vote with 48 per cent of the
vote against Mugabe's 43. However, the electoral laws said the
winner needed over 50 per cent of the vote, which meant that
Tsvangirai had just failed to win the presidency, and a second
round would have to be held. The date was set for 27 June.

I had campaigned for Mugabe and ZANU(PF) in the first round
and so I was agreeable to continue in the second round. I quickly

found out that the army were directly involved. They were openly threatening people if they did not vote for ZANU(PF).

At one election meeting, in Chief Mazviwha's area in Zvishavane, I was surprised to find myself sharing a platform with military commanders. I kept asking myself, "Is this the freedom we fought for?" One of the commanders was addressing the crowd and he had a pen in one hand and a gun in another. He told the audience that if they did not vote for ZANU(PF), they had better flee from their homes because the army would come looking for them. I remember that vividly. It was there that I made up my mind that I would never again participate in elections where people were openly threatened and intimidated into voting for any political party.

On 22 June, Tsvangirai announced he was withdrawing from the election to prevent further violence. The election went ahead – with Tsvangirai's name still on the ballot paper – and the results were announced two days later with Mugabe taking 85 per cent of the vote.

The result was almost universally rejected because of the violence, and it was clear that Mugabe would have to negotiate his way out of international isolation. South Africa's President Thabo Mbeki called on SADC to try to help find a solution. Talks began on July 25 and nearly two months later Mbeki announced that the basis for a deal had been concluded.

A government of national unity was to be formed, with Mugabe as president and Tsvangirai as prime minister. The negotiations continued, with frequent breakdowns, for many months, and it was only on 11 February the next year that the new government was sworn in.

Before the next elections in 2013, I had not considered campaigning again. I had retired from government.

However, shortly before the election I was visited by a group of officials from the ZANU(PF) election directorate. They said they had studied the preparations for the coming voting. They pleaded with me to campaign for ZANU(PF) in Zvishavane. "If you don't help us, ZANU(PF) will lose."

I agreed. I campaigned harder than I had ever before. When the results were announced I was happy to see that ZANU(PF) had won.

12

The CG Msipa Scholarship Trust

In 2008 President Mugabe was in the Midlands, and, as was the usual practice during his visits, I sat next to him in his car. I took the opportunity to tell him that he should not renew my appointment as governor because I wanted to retire and have a rest after many years of public service. This surprised him. He asked me why, noting that I was younger than he was. In reply, I agreed that I was younger – 77, against his 84 – but that the decision on when to take retirement was entirely personal. He agreed.

I must say, I expected him to tell me his plans for retirement too but he kept that to himself.

Early into my retirement I decided to do something that had always been close to my heart – to assist students from poor backgrounds with tuition fees.

The first time I did this was in 1957, when I was branch secretary of RATA. I approached members of the Indian business community in Kwekwe and one of them, a Mr Desai, offered to pay for one student for his entire secondary education at Goromonzi High School, just east of Harare, at the time one of a handful of government secondary schools for Africans.

The student chosen was one Boyman Mancama. After completing secondary school, he took a degree at the University of Zimbabwe, and after that studied for a BSc(Hons) at the University of London. After graduating, he started working in 1965 as a clerk for Shell, and moved five years later to Anglo American Corporation, where he eventually became executive director. At one time he was also my vice-chairman on the Agricultural Marketing Authority. Following his retirement he became an Anglican priest, and was a member of the board of the Shearly Cripps Children's Home, where he still serves. Mr Desai's generosity dramatically changed the course of Mancama's life, for which he was extremely grateful.

Throughout the years 1971 to 1979, I helped thousands of students to secure scholarships for educational studies through the Commonweath Fund as well as the United States Agency for International Development. As Midlands governor I found myself processing applications for Presidential Scholarships (instituted by President Mugabe's office) for young Zimbabweans to study at universities in South Africa. I read every one of the application letters and it was obvious that most of the applicants were deserving of financial assistance to continue their education. Only a few managed to get it, though. For the rest, I can only think their dreams must have been shattered. So I decided to complement them by launching another fund, in my name. The CG Msipa Scholarship Trust would specifically aim to assist intelligent but indigent students to attend local universities.

For this I had no money, but I was quite confident that the corporate world would rush on board to assist. My assumption was not completely correct.

Almost two years after the Scholarship Trust was first registered in 2009, the Mimosa platinum mining company came forward with a donation of $100,000 which allowed us to kick-start the operations of the Trust and to pay our first tuition fees in September 2011. The company funded students for engineering courses, and had first option on employing them after they graduated.

After that other donors began to come forward, though with smaller amounts. The official launch of the Trust in August 2012 was a big fund-raising dinner and dance in Gweru.

At the function, I dedicated the Scholarship Trust to my mother and all women of Zimbabwe in recognition of the fierce determination they have shown in the education of their children. Our country boasts one of the highest literacy rates in Africa and one of the main drivers of this success story is the determination of mothers to provide education for their children.

Since then, the Trust has been receiving applications almost daily. The students asking for financial assistance are mostly orphans, or children whose parents have lost their jobs or cannot get jobs because of the adverse economic environment.

I was pleased, however, that despite the economic hardships, we managed to pay tuition fees for over 200 students after the launch, many of whom would surely have dropped out of school if we had not assisted them.

By 2015 the Trust was supporting students at almost every university in Zimbabwe, pursuing degree studies of their choice and at universities of their choice. The demand remains overwhelming. Often we just don't know what to do in the face of it. Students come to us with high hopes and when we say, "Sorry, we have no money", some of them break down, as do their mothers who accompany them.

To create another source of funds, however modest, I donated 200 hectares of my farm just outside Gweru to the Scholarship Trust. The land was divided into two-hectare plots which were made available for sale to individuals. Part of the sale proceeds were used for providing infrastructure like roads and water, and the rest was set aside for the operations of the Trust. The response surpassed my expectations. The scheme turned into a retirement or holiday home for doctors, lecturers, company directors and senior police officers. Some of the stand owners purchased their plots from the United Kingdom, South Africa and Australia, where they were working. I named the settlement Sithabile Park, after my loving wife wife for 53 years until she died 2013. I hope that it will be a home of love, peace and friendship, for these were Charlotte Sithabile Msipa's virtues.

The Trust is involved in various fundraising activities, including a soccer trophy in the Premier League . It has become a major annual sports event, and there are plans to expand it. There is also an annual fund-raising dinner. I want the Trust to assist students long after I've gone. It is my fervent wish that the beneficiaries of the Trust will one day be able to help others in the same way that they have been assisted.

I have mentioned earlier that I went into teaching by choice, and then was literally forced out. Whenever I had a chance, I tried to do what I liked best – furthering education.

Reflections

My journey has been a long one but I'm happy that God has looked after me for all these years. Many of my colleagues have not lived as long as I have. When I was at Sunday school we used to sing, "Count your blessings, name them one by one and see what the Lord has done for you." The 84 years I have been around for are among those blessings.

But I have had little time to stand and stare. My life has been packed with action and anxiety, triumph and disappointment, as my generation was challenged to "unscramble" the "Scramble for Africa". From the late 1950s to the time we attained majority rule we watched the most extraordinary historical changes, not only in Zimbabwe but in the rest of Africa. I was there and I saw it happen and I participated in it. I belong to a generation of liberators.

After 84 years, I have decided to narrate what I did, with whom, and why I did what I did. It is time for reflections.

What comes to mind first are my parents who brought me into this world and nurtured me. They taught me the basics of life such as the need to work hard and to make friends and to live happily with other people. They also sent me to school. They had a clear vision for their children.

Cephas Msipa and his sons

My other blessing for which I shall always be grateful is the choice of my life partner, Charlotte. We got married in 1960 and she passed on in 2013 after 53 fulfilling years of marriage. She was special in every respect. She stood by me during hard times and during good times. I am what I am because of her. She taught me love, patience, tolerance, respect and friendship. She visited me in every prison where I was detained and never complained. Throughout the 53 years, she was a source of inspiration to me. She was proud to be a mother and a wife. Other things were secondary to her. She was a devout member of the Anglican Church where she made friends in Kwekwe, in Mufakose, in Hatfield and in Gweru. I respected her devotion to her church and she did the same for mine, hence my continued membership to the Church of Christ. She would remind me to go to church from time to time. The news of her passing away was received with disbelief and shock by friends and relatives. We were surprised to learn she had been declared a liberation heroine. On the burial day, President Mugabe and the First Lady, Grace, came to join the thousands of mourners at our home, at the church and at the Midlands provincial heroes' acre burial site. President Mugabe spoke glowingly about Charlotte's virtues. It was a most consoling message from an old friend. Joshua Nkomo would have expressed similar sentiments, and so would Simon Muzenda. I know they respected her more than they respected me. The Church of Christ in Windsor Park, Gweru, closed with the song, "How Great Thou Art",

Cephas Msipa with his wife Charlotte on their 50th Wedding Anniversary 28 August 2010.

I was greatly touched and humbled by the multitudes that came to pay their last respects to her. My old friend Hey Malaba (who celebrated his 94th year in 2014) said, "Cephas, you should accept that you will never see Charlotte again but remember the wonderful times you had together." It has taken me a long time to accept what Mr Malaba said. The void that she left in my life can never be filled. All I can do is to wish her eternal rest and to assure her that I shall always love her. The honour given to my wife is recognition of the enormous moral support given by many women and men who never aspire for positions in public life. They work behind the scenes and their influence moves the world.

Charlotte loved peace and she died peacefully. She loved others more than herself to the point where she cared about me more than herself. I am sorry that I did not do for her what she did for me, but we both kept our vows to remain together till death parted us. Her favourite prayer was:

God grant me the serenity to accept the things I cannot change,
the courage to change the things I can,
and the wisdom to know the difference.

Finally, to you who have taken the trouble to read about my long journey, I want to recall that during the struggle the cry was, "Freedom now". But how free are we, and are we using that freedom for the general good?

We promised the people that we were fighting for a Zimbabwe which would be a land of milk and honey. This implied prosperity and happiness for our people. Where is the milk and honey?

At independence both ZANU and ZAPU in their election manifestos promised, "equitable distribution of the country's resources". Is this happening? If not, why not? Why is the gap between the rich and the poor widening?

In the meantime I leave you with this: "Power corrupts, and absolute power corrupts absolutely". When we occupy positions of power, let us use that to enhance peace, prosperity and happiness for the majority of our people.

Epilogue

It is not easy to retire from politics just as it is not easy to retire from life, but I have chosen to observe political events from the terraces. Once in while I find it necessary to comment aware that the driving force behind my political involvement was the pursuit of freedom and justice.

Being a member of ZANU-PF, and before it ZAPU, NDP and ANC I have learnt a lot about the nature of politics and politicians. Some say the former is a struggle for power at every level, others that power corrupts and absolute power corrupts absolutely. ZANU-PF is a crucial part of the history of Zimbabwe and has been in power since 1980. However, by and large, ZANU-PF leaders and members seem oblivious to the critical bearing their conduct has on the nation, and particularly on the economy. ZANU-PF's conduct looms large in the minds of potential investors, and the constant upheavals and bickering within the party give the impression of instability. This does little to promote foreign direct investment or the growth of tourism. In addition, the fate of the late Ambassador Amos Midzi affords us a glimpse of the psychological and emotional toll borne by individuals and families affected by the internecine squabbles. Former friends shun each other and hate speech is used against those who belong to different parties. One begins to ask, "Is this the freedom we suffered and sacrificed for?"

Sometime in 2003 several senior members of ZANU-PF asked me to persuade President Robert Mugabe to name and groom the person who would eventually succeed him. These people were not wishing Mugabe to go; they were only saying that one day he will go, as is the way of all flesh. There were strong sentiments that such a move would limit internal strife in the party and guarantee a gradual, smooth transfer of power. The example of President Mwalimu Julius Nyerere's transfer of power in Tanzania was cited.

I was asked because colleagues knew of my long relationship with Mugabe and were convinced that I could discuss this delicate subject informally with him without causing any suspicion of wanting to take over from him.

I regret that I was unsuccessful in this bid as the president insisted that his successor would be democratically elected by ZANU-PF members through the appropriate party structures. In theory, Mugabe is correct, but in practice what he suggests may not work. I remain convinced that the current contentious approach to the succession is wasteful, destabilising and inappropriate for a country with such a fragile economy. If the past is anything to go by, the attempt to democratise the party has been met with hostility.

The first attempt to democratise the election of the top leadership of ZANU came in the form of the abortive Tsholotsho declaration which read inter alia:

1. That the country's four major ethnic groups, Karanga, Manyika, Zezuru and Ndebele should be represented in the presidium

2. That the position of a president should not be monopolised by one ethnic group but rotate among the four ethnic groupings

3. That the filling of positions in the presidium should not be by imposition by the party hierarchy but through democratic elections done by secret balloting

4. Such positions must be filled in accordance with the party constitution.

The presidium and politburo were determined to ensure the ascendency of Joyce Mujuru in 2004 even though they had to usurp the constitution of the party to do so. Mugabe's frustration in reaction to the Tsholotsho Declaration of 2005 was palpable, angrily he said, "There is everything wrong when chairpersons of the party meet secretly without the leadership of the party and worse still what would they be discussing there?"

His anxiety was apparent when he went on to say, "There is no party that runs like that. When the war was fought we fought as one on all fronts. We did not ask guerrillas where they came from but the newcomers are now saying this one comes from that region and that one from that ethnic group and so on. They should know we are non-tribalists and non-regionalists."

The tension that ensued led to a rupture as six provincial chairpersons and Jabulani Sibanda, leader of the Zimbabwe Liberation War Veterans Association, were suspended. The message was loud and clear – no one was to challenge the power of the president to install his anointed appointees into any position in the party hierarchy.

The expulsion and exclusion Joyce Mujuru and her perceived allies from ZANU-PF in December 2014 was, in reverse, a bizarre replay of her dramatic ascendency to the national and ZANU-PF vice presidency in 2004, which had the support from nine out of the country's ten provinces. In other words Mujuru was determined to be elected rather than appointed vice president in line with the party's constitution.

The doctrine of the single centre of power arose as Grace Mugabe was nominated to be the new secretary for the ZANU-PF Women's league. We must, however, remember that Joyce Mujuru was appointed vice president following the 1999 resolution by the League calling for the appointment of a female to the presidium. Nonetheless, in 2014 the gender issue was buried under a barrage of sensational publicity centred on unproven allegations of corruption, sabotage and assassination plots, and peppered with accusations of witchdoctors unleashing charms in favour or against certain named individuals. Mujuru and her allies were bludgeoned into retreat and were eventually expelled from the post-2014 ZANU-PF Congress.

President Mugabe recently urged party members to guard against those who wanted to rise to the top through unscrupulous means saying, "So you should watch. Watch out more of that trend. We now have some with unbridled ambitions – having ambition is not bad but we want unity." Meanwhile, the party's "own methods" are not crystal clear. For instance how does one measure the extent of "unbridled ambition" when attempts by ambitious aspirants to position themselves strategically for eventual succession are met with hostility? We need to find a way to reduce the tension in ZANU-PF succession politics as well as in our body politic. We know that tension and conflict are indications of social malfunction developing from uncontrolled competition. Politics can be regarded as a peaceful struggle for scarce resources, positions of influence and power and one in which the protagonists observe the rules applying to their interaction.

Stressed social relationships are characterised by hostility stemming from the perception that applicable rules or norms are not being observed. Once the levels of tension reach a certain level, conflict and disassociation follow. I therefore maintain that the people of Zimbabwe deserve better institutional arrangements than are currently on offer. The ZANU-PF constitution is a document of national interest that must be amended to allow for an orderly and predictable transfer of authority. In all this, Robert Mugabe has the power to remove causes of factionalism in ZANU-PF. That has been my call and it will remain my call.

Printed in the United States
By Bookmasters